ADVANCE PRAISE

"Ali Nasser draws on his seventeen years of experience advising entrepreneurs to lay out a roadmap for their unique balance sheets and help them make important life decisions. Many owners are searching for ways to bring it all together. This book provides the path."

—**DAN SULLIVAN**, Founder and President of Strategic Coach®

"Ali is the authority on entrepreneurial wealth. This book clearly articulates the core dilemmas all business owners face and brings them together with one integrated system. WISE™ is like EOS® for your personal wealth."

—**GINO WICKMAN**, author of *Traction* and *Entrepreneurial Leap*, creator of the Entrepreneurial Operating System (EOS), Entrepreneurial Leap, and Rocket Fuel

"Every business owner needs a guide to help navigate the decisions of business, wealth, and life. The Business Owner's Dilemma *provides a roadmap, and Ali is your guide."*

—**CAMERON HEROLD**, Founder of The COO Alliance and creator of the Invest In Your Leaders course and *Second in Command Podcast*

"As business owners, so much of our net worth and focus are tied up in our company. Ali lays out a roadmap for bringing the holistic financial picture together in a way that will discover—and best support—your unique personal goals."

—MARK C. WINTERS, co-author of *Rocket Fuel*

"The first time I heard Ali on stage, I was immediately riveted. He communicates profound truths but in a simple way to understand. Read this book and prepare to have your mind blown."

—KARY OBERBRUNNER, *Wall Street Journal* and *USA Today* bestselling author and CEO of Igniting Souls

"We have been using WISE for over five years along with Ali's coaching. This book integrates years of knowledge all in one place. It has a fantastic perspective on the entrepreneur's mindset during different phases of the entrepreneur's journey. The mindset at the start of the journey is different from the mindset towards the latter part of the journey. The "Entrepreneur's Investment Opportunity Diagram™" is profound. I make financial decisions all the time, but this model creates a new framework and perspective."

—VIMAL KOTHARI, Founder & President, Systel, Inc.

"An entrepreneur's guide to the universe. Every entrepreneur should read this book, it will have a lasting and meaningful impact on their journey from startup to exit."

—CORY JACKSON, CEO, CTG, Inc.

"Ali is a dynamic entrepreneur that truly cares about what he does and the community he serves. His insights and thoughtfulness about the challenges entrepreneurs face are unique not only in concept, but also in how they are communicated and solutions put into practice. This book helps the entrepreneurs be more intentional and capture what they have built."

—AMIN DHALLA, CEO, Houston Premier Radiology

"This is not another investment advice book; it is a blueprint to help you build a strong foundation that will support building a life strategy for your business as well as your personal vision. WISE is not a canned solution; it's a roadmap with Ali serving as a guide to help entrepreneurs find their best solution. I believe this book will be of great help to entrepreneurs."

—JORGE SQUIER, SVP Global Strategic Sourcing, board member and shareholder

"This book is an eye-opener for successful entrepreneurs to see the forest from the trees. Ali gives you the outside perspective to help you get a clear picture about what you really want."

—ASIF DAKRI, CEO, Wallis Bank

"This book is the Rich Dad Poor Dad of entrepreneurial wealth. Ali has developed a holistic process to systematically assess and organize your current and future life-business plans into an understandable roadmap. It showed me gaps that I didn't know existed and wouldn't have known until it was too late."

—JOSEPH BRAMANTE, CEO TriArc Real Estate Partners

"The Three Dilemmas™ are simply incredible. This book is the ultimate field guide for an entrepreneur's wealth."

—DAVE SPRAY, President & CEO, Export Advisors

"Improve your quality of life by having a holistic approach that allows you to plan all aspects of your financial life, reducing risk and uncertainty."

—HOWARD RAMBIN, CEO of Moody Rambin,
Personal Coach, Speaker

"The Business Owner's Dilemma provides proven solutions to the dilemmas that every entrepreneur faces as they achieve success in their business. I know it's a great book when as I read it I am highlighting, writing notes, and dog-earring pages for future reference. Such was the case with The Business Owner's Dilemma*! Kudos to author Ali Nasser for writing a book that is interesting and filled throughout with wisdom and insight sharpened through experience."*

—**JEFF HOLLER**, CEO, The Capital Chart Room LTD®

"Thoughtfully written and insightful guidance for entrepreneurs making once-in-a-lifetime decisions."

—**RICK WILSON**, managing director, Crutchfield Capital

"The concept of Return on Life Experience™ that Ali presents in The Business Owner's Dilemma *is nothing short of a major awakening for all successful entrepreneurs. The process of identifying what brings the most fulfillment and then laying a pathway to get there is a game-changer for all entrepreneurs."*

—**LORIE CLEMENTS**, EOS implementer and owner of
Springboard Solutions

the

BUSINESS OWNER'S DILEMMA

Take Control of the Mental Chatter,
Clarify Your Ideal Future, and Enjoy
the Success You've Earned

ALI NASSER

THE BUSINESS OWNER'S DILEMMA
Take Control of the Mental Chatter, Clarify Your Ideal Future,
and Enjoy the Success You've Earned

ISBN   978-1-5445-1658-5   *Hardcover*

        978-1-5445-0146-8   *Paperback*

        978-1-5445-0147-5   *Ebook*

        978-1-5445-0148-2   *Audiobook*

To Mom and Dad.
Thank you for being the most loving, humble,
and kind parents I could have ever asked for.

CONTENTS

A NOTE TO THE READER

IF YOU'RE AN ENTREPRENEUR OR BUSINESS OWNER, YOU'RE ONE of my favorite people on the planet. I am fascinated by the entrepreneurial mind, and I love digging deep to discover their core challenge and innovating ways to find the best path forward.

I have spent my career advising some of the most successful business owners on many aspects of their personal, business, and financial lives. I have been fortunate to see and hear their life experiences, victories, failures, regrets, and what they truly value most.

About ten years into my career, a few of those experiences motivated me to expand the impact of my work. In a short period of time, I had several engagements with business owners that had amassed tremendous amounts of wealth and were trying to gain clarity on how to best plan it all.

They had sold their companies and had levels of financial success that not only ensured security for themselves but for generations to come. Yet, amidst the financial freedom, they were not free from the mental struggles and financial dilemmas occupying their mind.

In fact, the challenges of constantly thinking about their dilemmas and not having a clear approach to truly address them were tremendously overwhelming.

I saw business owners who had spent a lifetime working to create freedom and independence but were not able to enjoy and experience the true benefits of their work.

Managing success and continuing growth was all-consuming and, in many cases, led to significant impacts on their physical health, mental health, and personal relationships. It was heartbreaking. Seeing individuals that had reached the summit of business success but did not have mental freedom terrified me. I was scared about my own mindset, health, and life experience. I clearly saw how I could end up in the same situation and how so many other owners were on this trajectory as well.

I became hyper-aware that wealth is a means, not an end.

Having worked with entrepreneurs at all levels and stages of business, I could clearly see the patterns that made this situation come to exist. The mindsets that entrepreneurs share, combined with the challenges of business success, create unique issues and opportunities, both for wealth planning and life planning.

I also saw how adjusting their approach and perspective could truly change the outcome for many business owners—and the earlier the adjustment, the more impactful the change.

Helping these business owners find clarity to their biggest wealth and life challenges gave me an increased sense of purpose. It made me realize the true value of the approach, system, and process that I had built. And it gave me a reason to further expand the knowledge beyond myself or my network.

WHAT YOU WILL LEARN FROM THIS BOOK

Before we dive deep into the content, philosophies, and approaches within this book, I want to be very clear about what this book is all about and exactly what you are going to get from reading it.

Business owners are going to face three critical dilemmas along their journey:

- The Re-investment Dilemma™

- The Legacy Dilemma™

- The Exit Dilemma™

To effectively address these dilemmas and their many associated decisions, business owners need a clear path.

This book introduces that path via the Wealth Integration System for Entrepreneurs™, or WISE™.

WISE is an approach and a framework for viewing all aspects of an entrepreneur's wealth. A proven system to bring all the pieces together through one lens. Creating a path to greater intentionality and integration.

There are six components within the system:

1. Balance Sheet Strategy™

2. Liquidity & Cash Flow™

3. Lifestyle & Legacy™

4. Exit Strategy

5. Asset Protection Strategy

6. Lifetime Tax Strategy™

Everything within the spectrum of a business owner's personal wealth will fit into one of these six components. Nothing is theoretical; WISE is a proven system that has been effectively implemented for successful business owners for over a decade.

It is important to note that WISE stands independent of any financial, investment, tax, legal, or business solution. Although the *W* stands for Wealth, it is not wealth in the traditional definition, which can often be associated with investments or portfolios. It is Wealth as a comprehensive collection of all your assets, plans, and personal values you hold dear.

The goal of the Wealth Integration System for Entrepreneurs is to provide business owners with better perspective so they are empowered to make better decisions.

This book is not a silver bullet. It does not tell you what decisions to make. It does not solicit or market any financial products or instruments. And it does not provide specific business, tax, legal, or financial advice.

This book was written primarily for established business owners and entrepreneurs that have already built a successful company. Generally, with a total net worth of $10 million–$100 million, inclusive of the market value of their company. With that being said, the concepts and content are relevant for business owners at all levels and can provide clarity and perspective at many stages of the entrepreneurial journey.

If you are facing one or all the dilemmas; if you are looking for how to bring it all together; if you want to maximize success and plan your life and wealth with intentionality—this book is for you.

Additionally, this book will be helpful to anyone that supports business owners. Professional advisors, coaches, spouses, family members, and successors are all parties that can benefit. This book will give you knowledge on how business owners think—their dilemmas, mindsets, and paradigms—and why understanding those differences changes the way we approach planning.

Throughout this book, I use the terms *business owner* and *entrepreneur*, sometimes interchangeably. I receive a lot of questions on the difference between the two, or why I used one term over another, so I want to explain this briefly.

Business owner refers to someone who currently owns and is leading an operating business. An entrepreneur may currently own a business *or* may have sold a business. If an individual sells their company, they may no longer be a business owner, but they are still an entrepreneur.

Owning a business creates a large impact on both wealth and life decisions; you will see many examples and stories of this throughout the book. However, underlying business ownership is the *entrepreneurial mindset* itself, which is often the driving force behind many decisions. This is why it is critical to consider the impact of both being a business owner and having an entrepreneurial mindset when planning your wealth and life.

Eighty percent of the people reading this book—maybe including you—are both a business owner and an entrepreneur. The other twenty percent may have exited their business or may have received their business stock from inheritance, sweat equity, or other means.

If you are an entrepreneur by DNA, you will always be one. This is the way you think. This is who you are. Your business may come and go, but the entrepreneurial mindset will stay.

YOUR GUIDE

For almost two decades, I have been committed to finding ways to enhance the lives and results of every business owner with whom I come in contact. It's my deep passion. As both a business owner and a guide working closely with business owners, I have learned that with the right perspective, decisions become easier and better.

If business owners can receive objective and thoughtful perspectives, their intentionality increases, which can often change their outcome altogether.

Business owners do not need to be *told what to do*. They need the options, guidance, and perspective so they can more clearly *decide what to do*.

My clients consider me as their Guide—and with your permission, I'd love to serve as your Guide throughout this book.

Through the content, I will show you so many aspects of entrepreneurial wealth. You will gain more clarity on what you have built, how you think, how to address your biggest wealth and life decisions, and the system that brings it all together.

The entrepreneurial journey is both motivating and challenging. It is one of the hardest and most rewarding paths one can choose. My hope is that what you learn from this book will help you capture and maximize your success. And not just maximize your return on investment but also your Return on Life Experience™.

With gratitude,

Ali Nasser

PART 1

DILEMMA

CHAPTER 1

THE THREE DILEMMAS™

*Framing Your Challenge Creates
the Path to Opportunity*

WHAT WOULD YOU TELL SOMEONE WHO HAS A $50 MILLION NET worth, entirely invested in Apple stock?

You'd probably tell them to diversify. They'd be crazy not to, right?

I could introduce my friend Justin to you in a similar way. His $50 million net worth is also in one company—but it's the company that he built. What would you tell Justin?

Would you congratulate him? Ask him if he planned to grow it to $100 million? Ask him what's next?

Why is that? Why would we tell the first person to diversify while celebrating the second? Does Justin's manufacturing company really carry less risk than Apple, one of the most successful companies of all time?

If you're an entrepreneur, you may already know the answer, or feel it intuitively—Justin has control, and we love control. **In fact, in situations where we have a sense of control, we visualize the opportunity far greater than we see the risk.** And the more successful we become, the greater our comfort for concentrated risk. Control makes it feel entirely logical for Justin to keep $50 million in his manufacturing company but unrealistic to invest the same amount in one stock.

Entrepreneurs are all very different in terms of the businesses they run and the choices they make, but underlying those differences is a commonality in the *way* they make those choices.

Most of us started building at a young age, with our first hustle beginning in our adolescent years. We were presented with some sort of challenge that we saw as an opportunity. Perhaps we wanted to prove ourselves to someone, to accommodate for something we lacked, to change what we had into something we wanted, or to just create something new. And we never really stopped. We continued to pursue opportunities, climbing bigger mountains and overcoming greater risks.

Years later, when we have a business that has become highly successful, we begin to face some key dilemmas.

The first is the Re-investment Dilemma™.

What should I do with profits? Re-invest back in the company, buy real estate, invest in the market, start a new company, or just save money in cash? What's the best strategy?

The second usually comes to mind a little later in life—the Legacy Dilemma™.

What is this all for? Family? Charity? Ego? Just for fun? How much is enough? What impact am I making? How do I ensure my children are empowered and not entitled?

The third is the Exit Dilemma™.

This could come at any point in time: What is my best exit strategy? Do I sell the company? When? For how much? What will I do next? Should I leave it to my children? Sell to my executive team? Will selling give me freedom of purpose or loss of purpose?

Every successful business owner will face one or all of these dilemmas over their lifetime, and, in many cases, all three at once.

The underlying question driving all of them is

"What is my best path forward?"

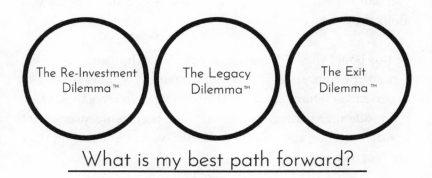

Plenty of authors, speakers, and mentors are available to help entrepreneurs grow their businesses. But once we have built the cash flow and equity that we dreamed of, what then?

How can Justin gain guidance on the best path for his $50 million net worth?

The reality is that traditional guidance was not created for the entrepreneur. They are a rare breed, especially at this level of success. Tax, legal, and financial solutions are usually built to address a specific need and often with a process to serve the masses as opposed to the exceptions.

The answers are rarely easy. Yours will depend on the stage you are in, the future you want, and the values you hold. **Furthermore, within these dilemmas exists both a wealth decision and life decision that needs to be addressed.** And having a system to gain clarity and perspective on all the different pieces will bring a much better outcome.

In other words, finding your best path forward is a journey, and you will benefit from a proven approach that helps guide you along the way.

In this book, you will learn about the Wealth Integration System for Entrepreneurs™ and how business owners that have experienced it have gained clarity on effective ways to address their dilemmas, bring all aspects of their entrepreneurial wealth together, and create the intention and integration they are seeking.

THE ENTREPRENEUR'S JOURNEY

Growing up in a family of entrepreneurs, I saw the joys, struggles, and challenges of business ownership from the inside. At the age of twenty, I started my first business and experienced how many long years of perseverance and hard work it takes to make a vision a reality—not to mention the risks involved in starting and running a company.

I have tremendous affinity, love, and respect for entrepreneurs who put everything on the line to build their vision.

Most entrepreneurs built their businesses from the ground up. They created something out of nothing, usually by working seven days a week for years while making many life sacrifices along the way. They did all of this while carrying boulders of risk and obligation. And when they finally reach their big milestones, they are often faced with heavy tax burdens and complex life decisions to navigate.

The rewards of business success can be tremendous. However, the sad part is that a very small percentage of entrepreneurs reach a high level of success. Approximately 65 percent of businesses will fail in the first ten years, and 75 percent will fail within fifteen. Of all small businesses, less than 20 percent make over $100,000 per year.[1] The majority of entrepreneurs who do accomplish success will not fully capture or monetize it. And many of those who do capture the monetary benefits of their business find it hard to enjoy the outcome of their work.

---

1   Source: US Bureau of Labor Statistics.

After so many years of intense work, it becomes difficult to slow down enough to enjoy what they have built, and many will spend years thinking and worrying about the next generation and whether they'll be equipped to succeed.

Without question, being an entrepreneur is one of the toughest roles there is—not only to reach any level of success but also to sustain, grow, and ultimately pass on the legacy to their loved ones.

Yet we do it anyway.

We each have our unique reasons. Perhaps we want our independence and an opportunity to create our own outcome, or we just love to build and grow. Your reasons might not be the same as mine, yet here we are—on our journey, wondering what mountain we are going to climb next.

I have spent over 20,000 hours consulting some of the most successful business owners on capturing their life's work and developing a strategy for their personal vision. I've seen and analyzed the patterns in mindsets, philosophies, and strategies across countless business owners, all while experiencing my own entrepreneurial journey.

The common denominator for us all, across every stage of the journey, is answering the question *What is my best path forward?* And **depending on where you are in your business, your life cycle, and your financial position, this core question will surface differently.**

I believe we are all looking for the same outcome: clarity of our purpose, alignment of our values, and peace of mind that there is an intentional plan in place.

To effectively reach this outcome requires many steps, including clarifying your desired life experience, truly understanding your wealth and what it can provide, and recognizing your new normal, or the opportunities that exist today that you may not have been aware of previously.

THE CORE ISSUE + THE PROVEN SYSTEM

Business owners don't walk into a CPA or financial advisor's office to ask them to solve a core dilemma. They want to know how to save money for April 15 or how to invest their excess capital. That's all the traditional planning approach asks us to do—to work with several individual professionals, each in their own silo, and go with the best option they have to offer for their specific expertise.

You likely have a plan from several of these people already, each drafted in various stages of your entrepreneurial journey and based on your goals at the time you established them.

When I entered the wealth advisory industry, I was shocked to see just how little advising advisors actually did. More accurately, they were often brokers, portfolio managers, or insurance agents, each operating within a model that works for the bulk of their clients.

Over time, I fell in love with helping the business owner gain clarity and perspective. This was more important to me than offering an investment or financial product. As I listened to their underlying concerns and understood their challenges, I wanted to create something better—both for myself and for all entrepreneurs. **We didn't need better products. We needed a better perspective of our wealth in general.** I knew that by creating better perspective, business owners could be empowered to make better decisions.

I noticed common paradigms that entrepreneurs had formed, some to their benefit and some to their detriment—and over the years, I've seen how realigning and reframing these paradigms creates a positive impact on their outcome and, in some cases, changes the outcome altogether.

The more specifically I was able to meet those needs, the more my role shifted from advisor to something else. I have been called by many titles—a coach, an advisor, a confidant, a quarterback, and a family CFO. I have been a resource that business owners can turn to for guidance on the most important business, life, and wealth decisions. Someone that knows their desires, their family, and their dilemmas and can help create the outside perspective to help them find their best path forward.

Over time I became a Guide, providing perspective, insight, and options so business owners could more clearly decide what they wanted to do.

I spent years practicing this different approach to serve my relationships. And through it, created a new framework to think about their wealth and life decisions.

Since business owners are so similar in mindset and life challenges, a system and approach began to emerge and, eventually, stood on its own to become the Wealth Integration System for Entrepreneurs, or WISE™.

By that time, the actual services that supported the strategy—the investment portfolio, the legal documents, the tax returns—all became more of a commodity. The value shifted toward the approach, the process, the collaborative professional team, and the way it all integrates together for the business owner.

I've been blessed to work with great business owners and great professional advisors that believed in the vision of creating an integrated and intentional strategy. By bringing the entire team of professional advisors together, aligned to the vision of the owner, and utilizing the framework of WISE, we were able to better collaborate and ensure the greatest value creation for the business owner.

The Wealth Integration System for Entrepreneurs addresses two distinct components for a business owner: a Life Decision and a Wealth Decision.

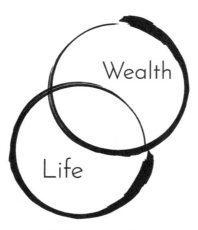

The system has been built and effectively implemented for business owners with $10 million–$100 million of personal net worth, including the fair market value of their business. With that being said, the principles, concepts, and considerations can be relevant to owners of all levels.

Wealth does not have a minimum, limit, or single definition. People interpret it in many ways, so we have to begin by aligning our definition of wealth. WISE defines wealth as everything that you've built that's of value—businesses, investments, assets, philosophies, and whatever else you hold dear and hope will carry on long after you're gone.

Creating integration for your wealth means bringing all the pieces together: assets, vision, family, professional advisors, charitable goals, and philosophies.

By bringing all the pieces together, we create the ultimate leverage and more options for value creation and preservation than most entrepreneurs realize is possible.

To be true stewards of wealth, we must include the money as well as the vision and values that helped build it.

WISE doesn't prescribe a preferred path forward. It helps each business owner find *their own* best path forward. It provides a framework for you to see the entire picture of what you have built and what you want to do with it.

With better perspective, better decisions come easily.

In other words, we are removing traditional solutions from the strategy. WISE stands independent of any money management, legal, tax, or financial service. We're stepping back to create a process and a framework instead of cobbling together products and documents, allowing your vision and underlying dilemmas to take center stage.

When you dig down deeper than surface concerns, something inside of you wakes up and reminds you why you are here in the first place—your purpose and true vision comes into focus. That vision then becomes the driver, simplifying and clarifying your decision points.

You are great at being a business owner and entrepreneur. There is no reason you should have to become an accountant, a lawyer, or a financial planner as well. Instead, let's learn how to apply your existing mindset and skill to create an integrated wealth strategy with the right people and process in place. Let's tailor it to the unique position and opportunities you have as a successful entrepreneur.

Let's help you find your best path forward.

CHAPTER 2

UNDERSTANDING THE ENTREPRENEUR'S MINDSET

You Stand Out, Don't Try to Fit In

TRADITIONAL INVESTMENTS ARE OFTEN DEFINED IN TERMS OF a portfolio that can be divided into percentages of stocks, bonds, and cash. That concept typically appeals to someone who works for a company and is saving for retirement, but entrepreneurs generally don't relate to that kind of thinking. They don't think of wealth in terms of asset allocations and portfolios of stocks and bonds.

Entrepreneurs see wealth in a very different way.

For most entrepreneurs, their single biggest and most important investment is their business. Many have the majority of their net worth tied up in the company they created and feel quite comfortable with that level of concentration.

This key difference between business owners and traditional investors should make an enormous impact on all aspects of their planning. It should also create tremendous opportunities, but it's a difference that is largely unaddressed by traditional methods.

To best plan for this concentrated position, we have to understand the mindsets that shape them in the first place. Let's look at the two primary factors that set entrepreneurs apart: control and risk.

CONTROL AND RISK

Entrepreneurs love control. Without it, we almost suffocate. As a result, we are more likely to take on a risky situation where we have control than to stay in something stable where we don't. It's a natural, unique desire we have to control our own future, for better or worse.

Control is the entrepreneur's ability to make a change and adapt to any situation to create the potential outcome they desire.

When you own your own company, you have a very high level of control. You can determine whether you want to shut down a product line, take on a customer, move locations, hire and fire staff, launch new products, and more.

Rightly or wrongly, the entrepreneur assumes their business is not as risky merely because they can control it.

In the introduction, we compared the $50 million of Justin's company to having $50 million invested in Apple. For Justin, investing in his own company seems low risk because of the control he has over the organization. He can see both opportunities and challenges on the horizon, so he knows what's coming. He knows what accounts payable and accounts receivable look like. He knows what his customers need. His perception of risk is low because of the confidence he has in himself to make the right decisions for the business.

Because of this inherent need for control, investing in public companies looks very different to the entrepreneur than an investment in themselves or their own company. With investments in the stock market, there's nothing an investor can do to affect the way a public company functions or to influence the decisions the CEO makes. If an individual investor doesn't approve of a public company's management team, they have little or no recourse. Additionally, an entrepreneur cannot influence the stock markets, and they're probably going to be too small of an investor to get a seat on the board or to make an impact through voting shares.

	Stock Market	Your Business
Control	LOW	HIGH
Perceived Risk	HIGH	LOW

Combining the lack of control with the volatility that markets often have, most entrepreneurs perceive investing in the stock market as high risk—even in ways that a professional advisor would otherwise consider low risk.

This lack of control is often why many entrepreneurs have a bad first experience in the market. They usually like to make a concentrated investment, just like they did in their business, and when they see the value fall, the only thing they can control is hitting the sell button. This results in a negative experience that often taints their view of investing in anything other than what they control. We will expand upon this in the chapter on Balance Sheet Strategy™.

RISK MEETS LIFE CYCLE

Entrepreneurs conceptually weigh opportunities and risk every day. You know what moves the needle and what opportunities to pursue without much of a formula or spreadsheet. If something hits your desk that's more urgent, or if an opportunity comes along that carries more promise, you'll pivot. It's what makes you great at building a business, and it's instinctual rather than mechanical.

Business risk comes in many forms and sizes—it's not just the downside risk based on economic factors. It could be that your business is potentially exposed to disruption, and you could be marginalized by some new technology or new business model. It could be that you've reached a level of maturity where the business doesn't have the opportunity to grow at the same rate anymore.

Risk could also involve the owner being absent from the business due to a health problem, incapacity issue, family conflict, or even passing away. Key employees or customers could also leave the company, resulting in a very different business situation or value than you've experienced to that point.

The challenge is that, as entrepreneurs, we have a skewed perception of risk within our business because of the control we have over it. In fact, an actual risk/return measurement is rarely analyzed.

If risk were made measurable, the business owner could make a more informed decision, and the chances are high that it could become a different decision than they initially expected to make. In other words, **if an owner could more clearly see the true return and risk of their business, they would be empowered to make better and more holistic decisions.**

To gain perspective on how much to invest in your company versus your personal balance sheet, think about the decision from three angles: where you are in the business cycle, where you are in your life cycle, and your personal desire for risk.

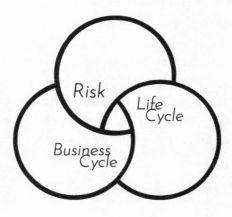

Every business goes through the same general growth phases, often called the "business cycle." It starts with proof of concept—is your service or product viable? Then you reach startup growth, where you are having fun closing deals and making magic happen. Next, you hit the challenges of scale, where you need to revisit your systems, processes, and people. Eventually comes steady growth and expansion, and finally, you will reach maturity. Once in maturity, you will either have to innovate to continue growth or face a gradual decline.

Each person's individual life cycle in relationship to the business has its own predictable pattern as well. This first phase is growth, over perhaps ten to twenty years, where an owner is all-in. Their business represents 90 percent of their net worth and 200 percent of their emotion. Generally, an owner bootstraps their way through these growth years, working many hours per week and looking forward to the day when the company can be self-running so they can have freedom of time and money.

The second phase is acceleration. Here, the company is generating much more cash flow, and the owner is building a personal balance sheet from profits and might be shifting to a more manageable work/life pace.

Finally, the third major phase is focused on capture, where an owner has experienced great success. They want to continue to grow but are also considering taking chips off the table. Family, lifestyle, time, health, and appetite for risk all play heavily here and can change the business owner's desired path forward.

In addition to the phase you are in, consider your unique desire for risk. If the business did fail, do you want to start again? That conversation may be very different with owners who are in their thirties or forties compared to those who are in their sixties or seventies.

In a later stage of life, you may not have the same desire to be as fully invested in the business as you were decades earlier. You may want to have enough capital separate from the company to ensure your financial independence.

I often hear owners in the later stage of the life cycle say things like, "I want to be fully engaged in my company and grow it, but I also want to take enough chips off the table that if anything bad ever happened to the company or me, I'd have financial stability."

Alternatively, a business owner who is thirty-five years old and has built a multimillion-dollar technology company might not be opposed to the idea of being all-in and fully invested. They might just need enough capital on the side that could allow them to restart a new company if something were to go wrong with their core business.

Everybody is unique.

There are younger business owners who are more risk-averse and eighty-year-olds who desire "all-in" growth by any means necessary. As a result, there is no cookie-cutter advice for entrepreneurs—risk measurement always relates to the individual business owner's particular opportunity sets, desire for risk, and stage in business and life cycle. Considering all those components together is what creates an initial framework to address wealth and life decisions.

THE PARADIGM OF MONEY™

The traditional thought behind strategic planning is simply to get you from Point A to Point B. People and organizations across the world use this as a descriptor every day: *Point A is where you are, Point B is where you want to be, and we can build a plan to get you there.*

Well, not so fast. There is also Point C™ to consider.

Point C is where you *think* you are. **And there can be a huge difference between where a business owner "thinks they are" and where they actually are.**

This can create a large challenge when understanding and executing personal planning decisions because there is often a misalignment between perception and reality. This is especially true with wealth and money.

Steven Covey, in his book *The 7 Habits of Highly Effective People*, explored the notion of paradigms. Paradigms are like an imprint that we capture of a particular situation that often sticks with us. A simple example of this is first impressions.

In the past, you've met someone that made a great first impression. They made you feel happy and valued, and chances are every time you think of them, your subconscious brain tells you how great they are—all from an initial encounter. The more emotional the experience, the more powerful the paradigm. Once a paradigm has been formed, it can be difficult to change, and, in some cases, even impossible. Hence the old saying "You never get a second chance to make a first impression."

This holds exceptionally true when it comes to money. For many reasons, money is highly emotional. And we all have a Paradigm of Money that was likely formed at a young age.

To discover and explore yours, think about the following question:

What is your earliest memory of money? Take a minute to think about it. Once you have identified that memory or memories, think through the experience and emotions. Is your experience one of abundance? Scarcity? Did it come easy? Was it painful?

MEMORY

_____

_____

_____

FEELINGS

_____

_____

_____

I was meeting with a business owner that had recently sold his company for nine figures. More money than he ever needed and enough that could retire his family for generations. He was having a lot of struggles with planning his wealth and family legacy and was looking for a breakthrough of some kind. I will never forget what he told me:

> Ali, my first memory of money was not having any. I remember sitting on the sidewalk with my mother's arms wrapped around me in the freezing cold because we didn't have the money to pay rent.
>
> It was the most painful experience of my life, one that I never want to experience again.

The raw emotion he expressed from the answer brought tears to his eyes and mine. His Paradigm of Money was one of extreme scarcity, and regardless of what financial circumstances he was under today, that early experience impacted everything.

This information entirely changed the approach to planning his wealth. His Paradigm of Money was one of not having enough, having to start working at a young age and provide for his family.

The next contributor to your Paradigm of Money is your most impactful financial experiences over your lifetime. One business owner was heavily invested in the Texas real estate market in the 1980s when there was an oil glut, every savings and loan institution was failing, real estate tanked, and his leveraged real estate portfolio became worthless. He watched his fortune go from over $20 million in 1980 to zero by 1984.

Today, when he hears about oil prices plummeting, what do you think his subconscious response is?

You got it, the risk of losing everything.

Every decision that he makes starts from protecting that downside risk and having extreme caution with debt.

Your Paradigm of Money is based on your early memories combined with your most impactful experiences. Together they create your viewpoint and contribute toward how you invest, how you see your position, and how you take risk.

Most highly successful entrepreneurs built something out of nothing. And oftentimes, their early memory of money was not one of ease and abundance but one of challenge or scarcity. In some cases, this contributed to their drive to build something. However, once it is built, it's very hard for them to see the reality of their present situation because they spent so many years building habits and subconscious thoughts based on prior circumstances.

This all manifests when one day you are faced with having to make decisions about what you want to do with all of your success.

You may have reached a point where you have more than you will ever need. You might have resources today that could substantially change your lifestyle, how you spend your time, your levels of stress, or your responsibility. You likely have opportunities that you may have been entirely unaware of. But addressing your best path forward requires you to see your current position with greater clarity—a position that is likely very different from Point C, or "where you think you are."

If for forty years your paradigm was "I have to work hard to move forward, and if I'm not moving forward, I'm moving backward," it is going to take some time and intentionality to make the shift you desire. However, making that shift can be life-changing.

WISE helps business owners create awareness of their paradigms, perspective of their current situation, and clarity on their desires for the future.

Having better perspective on these items will enable better decisions. And **it's not just about making financial decisions that yield a great return on investment but having those decisions support a great Return on Life Experience™.**

At the end of the day, wealth is a means, not an end. A means to create an outcome. The outcome may be lifestyle, social impact, freedom, security, fun, or even competition.

My goal is to help create the perspective for business owners to see their situation with a new lens, communicate the opportunities that can help capture their success, and motivate them to increase intentionality and find their desired life experience.

ENTREPRENEURS DON'T RETIRE™

The concept of retirement planning for entrepreneurs is quite flawed. Creating a plan for when you'll sell your company, stop working, golf, socialize, and travel the world—it's more than likely not going to happen. The reality is that most Entrepreneurs Don't Retire. Not because you can't, but because you don't *want* to. You want to live your life's purpose, and that often involves actively using your talents and abilities for as long as you can.

If you choose to sell your company, you might spend a few months relaxing before you realize you have been an entrepreneur because you love to build things and make progress. I've witnessed this firsthand with many business owners. They simply don't retire. Instead, they move on to something new.

This is not to say that retirement doesn't happen, but it's the exception rather than the rule, especially for the owner-founder.

Most of you reading this book already know whether you're a person who doesn't want to retire. I can relate. I'm confident I'll always be working toward something. I love what I do, and I couldn't sit still if I tried. If you do not know the answer yet, your spouse will—if he or she laughs at the idea of you retiring, you can take it as gospel.

Rather than trying to fit into the common model of retiring at age sixty-five and collecting an annuity and a Social Security check, your planning and thinking around retirement should match your unique planning and thinking as an entrepreneur.

Instead of being able to stop working, you probably just want to refocus on freedom of time—a future where you can apply yourself to whatever entrepreneurial venture you desire, regardless of the level of revenue or profit.

There are two key concepts that can really help in thinking about all of this: the Point of Optionality™ and your Return on Life Experience.

Some entrepreneurs have reached a point where what they have built is worth more than what they will ever want for their desired lifestyle. If they sold their company, they would never have to work another day in their life.

They could pursue whatever passion, business, or endeavor that their heart desires, regardless of what financial impact it would make. I call this the Point of Optionality. And many who have reached this point don't even realize it.

On the other hand, almost everyone is painfully aware that time is finite. We all get 24 hours in a day and 365 days in a year—the choice is how to use that time.

There are many ways to capture your business success that help you to increase your return on investment. However, for many entrepreneurs, there is something even more valuable than return on investment, and that's the Return on Life Experience.

The choices we make about how we spend our time, how we think, and who we are with collectively make up our life experience.

How we allocate our time is one of the most powerful ways to impact our Return on Life Experience.

Time and money are deeply connected, and the more money you accumulate, the more intentional you can be with your time.

Think of it this way: if you had all the financial resources to reallocate your time in whatever way you desire, what would you do?

Chances are you would still build something, maybe keep building your current business, but would the *way* you build it change? Would the way you spend your time change?

In your ideal world, how many days a year would you be working? How many days traveling? How many days unallocated? What would you do with loved ones? Do you have a bucket list? Do you have passions, hobbies, or interests that you haven't had the time to pursue?

Most entrepreneurs have never truly thought about these questions because we have been so consumed by building our business.

Creating intentionality with both time and capital will increase your Return on Life Experience.

Regardless of where you are in the entrepreneurial journey, repositioning your time and capital to align with your desired life experience is one of the most powerful exercises you can do.

As I take you through the WISE journey, you will see how each of the components come together to support your vision and will help you create your desired Return on Life Experience.

CHAPTER 3

THE ISSUES WITH TRADITIONAL PLANNING

*Why Mass Market Doesn't Serve
Top Performers*

WHEN I WAS A TEENAGER, I WAS PASSIONATE ABOUT PLAYING basketball. Usually five to seven hours a day, two hours of morning practice, an hour and a half after school, and three hours in the evening. It reached a point where the sound of a ball bouncing was normal background noise for my family.

Over time, I developed debilitating knee pain, tendonitis, and severe inflammation in both knees—beyond what one might expect from merely playing hard. The doctors told me I needed surgery, and, trusting their opinion, I went ahead with it. After the procedure and recovery period, the knee pain returned, just as bad as before. Eventually, it forced me to stop playing basketball.

In the years that followed, I tried everything to cure it. I went to many doctors who seemed all too ready to prescribe cortisone shots or rounds of anti-inflammatory pills and painkillers. Still, no real progress.

Many years later, in my thirties, it was a personal trainer and physical therapy expert who finally helped me find relief. I knew deep down that the medication only treated my *symptoms* but did nothing to address the core issues causing the pain. If we really wanted to make progress, we would have to figure out and treat the cause.

After a full body assessment, we actually found several potential causes that had combined to create that level of recurring pain. Running with my quads, using incorrect form when training, and not activating my glutes had put excess, unnecessary pressure on my knees and caused the injury.

He adjusted my form, designed an exercise regimen to strengthen my glutes, gave me training on how to use a foam roller, and suggested I see a nutritionist to revamp my diet to reduce the inflammation in my body. When I made structural, physical adjustments to bring my body into alignment, the majority of my problems went away.

Those exercises, stretches, and habit changes corrected the errors that created the pain and injury in the first place. Over the months and years that followed, my knee pain gradually decreased, and I went from needing ice and painkillers after any sports or exercise to rarely needing ice and never needing a painkiller.

Eventually, I was able to run and play sports with very low levels of pain. I became acutely aware of imbalances in the body, which allowed me to prevent or better manage future injuries.

After all those years of treatment after treatment, including expensive and painful surgery, *one person* was able to bring me into alignment using relatively simple techniques.

More recently, I read Tom Brady's book, *The TB12 Method,* which, in short, creates a roadmap for physical longevity, injury prevention, and maximizing your body's output for the specific demands of your activities or sport(s). TB12 is Brady's system that holistically addresses physical health, including exercise, anti-inflammatory diet, and the missing piece of traditional sports training—pliability.

When I read the book, I was constantly reminded of how the traditional training methods were broken, and hearing it from one of the greatest athletes of all time who had access to the most advanced methods on the planet was eye-opening. Even at Brady's level of training exposure, he had to shift from the traditional paradigm to create a better outcome. The result was sustained peak performance.

Looking back, if I had some of the knowledge from Tom Brady's book, or my trainer, it would have likely prevented my knee injury and perhaps allowed me to further pursue my passion of basketball.

Similarly, entrepreneurs are often sold ways of treating their various financial, tax, and future planning problems as one-size-fits-all "treatments" or the "strategy of the year." Offshore trusts, sexy tax-driven investment programs, financed insurance policies to create free money, hedge funds with limited downside but all the upside, unicorn private equity deals, exclusive access but only with a high investment minimum, money managers that will always outperform the market, or "build your own family office, and that will help your problems go away." The list goes on and on, constantly changing with market trends and the latest consumer frustration. All remedies to give you a "fix" to the current problem.

I maintain that adjusting the right things at the top level makes 90 percent of the problems go away. It also allows you to be more focused, which might be the greatest benefit of all, as **unnecessary distractions and mistakes can be the biggest detractor to your growth.**

The challenge is that traditional planning methods are reactive in nature. Most professionals focus on specific solutions to current problems rather than strategic planning for your future. Furthermore, very few professional advisors have a client base that has reached these levels of success, and if they do, it's hardly the core focus of their business. They aren't used to the increased complexity and challenges, much less the unique mindset with which an entrepreneur shows up.

As a result, most professionals just seek to ensure that their specific component is well executed, as best they know how. And since there is no clear way for professionals to see the full picture, many issues and opportunities go unnoticed. This situation— while well intended and functional for the masses—can create serious inefficiencies for highly successful business owners.

In fact, when we understand the path that a business owner takes from early career to remarkable success—then layer on top of that the incredible odds they overcame in reaching those levels of success—it makes perfect sense that their plans no longer match their position.

It's worth noting here that my previous doctors were all trained, skilled, and experienced in treating symptoms. They just weren't practiced in addressing the core issue.

Let's take a closer look at the various professionals and plans that helped you get to where you are. And how the traditional approach to planning created a gap.

"I'M ALL SET"—WHY WE AVOID REASSESSING OUR PLANS

Most highly successful entrepreneurs say their planning is in good order—they have multiple advisors, each of whom provides respective tax, legal, financial, and insurance services; in addition, they may have a CFO or a COO that runs their business financials. For these entrepreneurs, it's natural to assume you don't need to do any more planning. I often hear this expressed in the phrase "I'm all set."

But each of these professional service providers works in silos, with their own plans for their own components and little way to assess the overlap. **This segmented approach often leads to major planning gaps, especially for those who have reached a high net worth.**

35

Usually, those gaps remain hidden until some type of catalyst uncovers them in dramatic fashion. It might be a huge increase in income, the sale of a company, a lawsuit, a death, or a divorce. And by the time that catalyst has come along, it's usually too late to fix the problem. The damage has already been done.

For many owners, this ends in disappointment or even tragedy for their family. Substantial amounts of their life's work, time, money, energy, and effort are wasted because of unaddressed planning. The higher the owner's net worth, the more impactful their losses can be. Furthermore, the negative outcomes can often affect family members, creating family conflict and damaged relationships.

I have found there are three common reasons someone will say they're all set: they don't know what they don't know, they don't want to prioritize planning, or they don't have trust.

You might have even been burned by bad experiences in the past, which makes you feel uneasy about starting anything new. Maybe you're just tired of people who try to sell you on their solutions without understanding your situation. Plus, planning takes work and requires you to think about things you often don't want to.

These are all completely understandable reasons for not wanting to reassess your plans. But the reality is that once you have substantially grown your company and your wealth, you have likely outgrown the traditional methods of planning.

PERCEPTION VS. REALITY

From the entrepreneur's perspective, multiple smart professionals are working on their behalf in different areas, so everything must be fine. But when we pull all of the different planning components together, a different picture emerges.

Let's use the analogy of pieces of a puzzle. The business owner sees they have a tax plan, legal documents, trusts, investments, insurance, and a business plan. In reality, when you bring all those pieces together, the puzzle pieces often do not fit. They were set up by different people, at different times, based on different goals. In short—the planning was segmented.

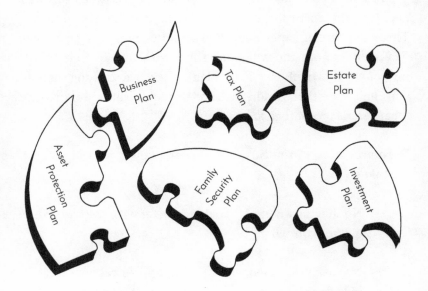

This is what disjointed wealth planning can look like. The fragmented pieces of the puzzle represent the isolated or incomplete planning, and the gaps in between represent the outcome of a segmented approach. Pieces of the puzzle can be replaced with trusts, entities, investment strategies, insurance policies, and legal documents that are outdated and misaligned with the entrepreneur's priorities.

Adding to this complexity, the business owner has become substantially more financially successful than when they first established those plans, further exacerbating the issues created by segmented planning.

There's no need to wait for a catalyst moment to sweep through and test the fortitude of your wealth plans and structures. Through years of experience, I've seen the common gaps business owners have and will share them with you. Keep in mind, my goal in this book is to bring light to the overarching themes and challenges that owners face and not get too granular in technical details or strategies.

Here are some of the business owner's key gaps and biggest mistakes:

- Not having a complete balance sheet with the true value of your company.

- No cash flow management or liquidity strategy—treating all your capital as though it is one big pot with no defined structure, purpose, or strategy.

- Making isolated investment decisions—not measuring your opportunity cost or unintended consequences. ("This deal looks good, let's do it.")

- Having the tax tail wag the dog—making decisions heavily driven by tax benefit or perceived tax savings.

- Not having an exit strategy in mind for your business, even if you do not have a current plan to exit.

- Reactive tax planning for April 15—trying to maximize savings right before you file your return and not having a plan to strategically minimize your lifetime tax.

- Underestimating the value of *you*. You are the central part of your business and plan. The impact of you not being around is substantial, and not just financially.

- Making decisions based on where you started vs. your new position and new normal. Limited thinking based on prior resources and obstacles.

- Not planning for your life after you sell the company and thinking that reaching the summit of your mountain is the end goal.

- Thinking that business succession is a document or an event and not a process.

- Not having an investment strategy that has long-term sustainability.

- Investing money with multiple money managers and hedge funds trying to outperform the market.

- Leaving money on the table when you exit your company and not capturing your full value.

- Constantly focusing on your gross return and not your net return.

- Planning your estate and investments as though you will always be there to run them and not thinking about what your family or heirs can handle.

- Having a segmented advisor team, working on big plans and big numbers with no overarching strategy, and you having to pull all the pieces together.

- Not having a capital structure or strategy to fund your plans for growth and expansion.

- Not planning for liability exposure, underestimating the value of an asset protection strategy for you and your wealth.

- Not having a plan for family financial continuity.

These are just some of the strategic-level issues that I see very commonly within entrepreneurial wealth. The Wealth Integration System for Entrepreneurs takes all of these items and organizes them into six components, then helps you develop a strategy for each.

In Part 2, Design, I'll show you how those components bring the pieces of the puzzle together with your goals to create the outcome you desire.

The bottom line is that you have these gaps and issues because of your growth and success, not because of any fundamental or unique oversight. It's a normal part of your growth, and it's natural to feel overwhelmed that so many areas of your planning may need reassessment. Remember, you are part of a fraction of 1 percent of business owners. And that level of success requires some reassessment.

To complete the virtual assessment and get clarity about your current position, go to www.wiseglobalnetwork.com/assessment or scan the QR code below.

SUCCESS REQUIRES REASSESSMENT

Before we continue, take a moment to appreciate what you've built. Often, as entrepreneurs, we get so caught up in what we *didn't* accomplish that we forget to give ourselves credit for what we *did*.

It took an enormous amount of blood, sweat, and tears to get where you are.

Small business is the growth engine and the economic driver for the entire country. In the United States, 70 percent of jobs are created by the 4 percent of the population who are willing to take big risks to build something.

Think about your company and all the jobs that it creates—not only for your employees but also all of the surrounding service providers and vendors with whom you do business. You support so many people in so many ways, and that's something to celebrate. You've made a positive contribution to society and the world. And you're in rare company.

Fewer than 20 percent of businesses make $100,000 of profit per year. If your profit is north of $1 million, you're in the top fraction of a percent of annual income—not just in the United States but in the world.

You've accomplished a level of success that most people only dream about, and once upon a time, what you dreamt about. Embrace that success. Acknowledge what it required. You did exactly what you needed to get to this point.

Now that you have reached this level of success, you'll require an equal level of care in planning it.

When you're focused on the growth of your business, personal planning is often set aside. You're constantly thinking about what it will take to survive and grow, and since you've always been a builder, planning and managing your success is not always in your DNA. However, **you have reached a point when planning what you have built becomes as important as, or more important than, just growing it.**

At this stage, your success requires reassessment. Capturing your business success necessitates a proactive versus reactive approach.

SO WHAT IS IT THAT YOU TRULY WANT?

Take a moment to really think about it. Write it down. What are the three most important outcomes you want?

_____

_____

_____

You may want to capture your success in some way. Perhaps you want to bring all the pieces together. And you likely want the fewest steps to the best possible outcome.

You might be thinking about how your wealth can create the best life experience and impact on what you value most.

If you're ready for a more proactive approach to planning, WISE will give you the perspective you want to create clarity on your best path forward.

PART 2

DESIGN

CHAPTER 4

THE WEALTH INTEGRATION SYSTEM FOR ENTREPRENEURS™

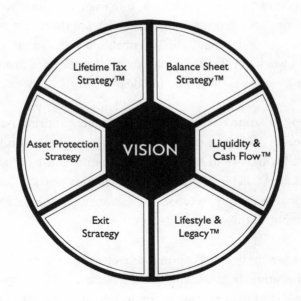

EARLY IN MY CAREER, I REMEMBER READING A PASSAGE IN THE book *The E Myth* by Michael E. Gerber. To paraphrase, it said that systems permit ordinary people to achieve extraordinary results. However, without the use of systems, even extraordinary people find it hard to produce ordinary results, predictably.

I loved the quote but questioned how that was possible while still addressing the unique situations that so many of my clients faced. Having a system may help, I conceded, but how do we build customization for the individual? That question quickly turned into a challenge: how can we effectively create an accelerative system while keeping the details bespoke to a particular person, situation, and background?

After working with entrepreneurs year after year, I started to notice the entrepreneur's mindset. Not only did they share concerns and thought processes, but many of them were also looking for some type of comprehensive solution. A way to see all the pieces come together. The problem wasn't that a system wouldn't work but that nothing existed that catered to an entrepreneur's personality, needs, and desires.

As a stopgap, some entrepreneurs hire their children to manage their wealth and their estate. Other entrepreneurs build their own family offices and hire their own teams. Some put more on an individual trusted advisor like an attorney or CPA than their role allocates, simply because the owner was looking for some way to bring all the pieces together.

Still others simply take it upon themselves to manage all of their wealth because they just can't find a comprehensive system or structure. It always seems easier to stick with what you've always done than it is to learn how to use something new.

Entrepreneurs use systems to level up in every other part of their world. There comes a time when you have to apply that same mindset to your planning as well.

WISE™ puts a framework around the full picture, both your life goals and your total financial position, including your business. A big-picture view of the puzzle. Having this better perspective allows you to make more holistic decisions.

The common issues with traditional planning that we identified in the last chapter relate directly to the six components of WISE. Everything in the spectrum of entrepreneurial wealth fits into one of these six areas. They are

1. **Balance Sheet Strategy™.** This is the overarching investment strategy for your entire balance sheet. It defines your combination of business investment, private equity, public equity, real estate, fixed income, and cash. It is important because it allows you to holistically view assets, returns, risk, and opportunity cost.

2. **Liquidity & Cash Flow™.** This is the way you position, distribute, manage, and use all of your cash. It includes your working capital in the company, your salary, bonus, distributions, and all of your savings and passive income streams, both business and personal. It is important because everything starts and ends with cash flow.

3. **Lifestyle & Legacy™.** This is all of the capital you have on your balance sheet specifically allocated to a certain goal. Is this Lifestyle Capital—spending, investing in deals, living, and enjoying? Or is this Legacy Capital— your children, your beneficiaries, or your charitable intentions? The distinction is important because it

defines the specific goal for each part of your wealth, which will directly impact how you view and position it.

4. **Exit Strategy.** This includes sale, succession, and continuity—the three eventual paths your business can take. Exit through a sale of your stock. Succession of your stock to a family member or management team. Continuity of your company in the event of the unexpected. This is important because it is likely the largest asset on your balance sheet and highly connected to you.

5. **Asset Protection Strategy.** This is the plan you have to protect everything you have built. Protecting assets against lawsuits and risks, planning for uncertainty, insurance, and risk management. It is important because it helps you identify and protect what you have built and the associated risks.

6. **Lifetime Tax Strategy™.** The plan to bring all of your goals together with the first five components of WISE in the most tax-effective method. And not just for one tax year, but for your entire lifetime. It is important because your largest bill is to the IRS, and being intentional with a tax strategy can allow you to keep more of what you have built.

In order to build a plan for each of these components, you will need to get clear about your goals. And not just high-level goals such as "I want to grow and preserve my wealth" or "I want to minimize my tax burden," but specific goals that have measurable outcomes and can be planned for. Goals that you, your professional advisors, and family can support.

At this point, you have clarity on why planning for the business owner is so different; the Re-investment Dilemma™, the Legacy Dilemma™, and the Exit Dilemma™ that owners face on their journey; and how it all ties to one core question: what is my best path forward?

You've learned about the entrepreneur's mindset toward control and risk, how the traditional approach to planning doesn't fit the owner's unique situation, and how everything in the universe of entrepreneurial wealth fits into one of the six components of WISE.

Next, I'll guide you through each of the components and share stories of how WISE concepts and tools have been used to create greater clarity and perspective as you climb your entrepreneurial mountain. I'll then share with you the proven process to actually execute a strategy to bring everything you have built together under one plan, creating more purpose behind all of your wealth.

CHAPTER 5

BALANCE SHEET STRATEGY™

The Lens That Helps You See
Clearly and Confidently

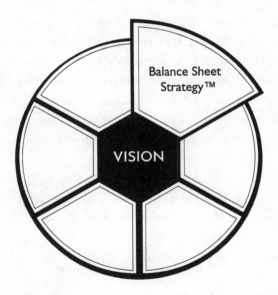

IN AN EARLIER CHAPTER, WE DISCUSSED HOW CONTROL PLAYS A huge role in the entrepreneur's perception of risk. We discussed how Justin has $50 million in his manufacturing company and how that seems entirely reasonable versus $50 million invested in Apple stock.

It's this appetite for concentrated risk that creates the outsized returns, or losses, that many entrepreneurs experience. There is no way a business owner would put all their money in someone else's company the way they would put it in their own; and when you add debt, personal guarantees, all the emotion, and all the loss of sleep, it's a huge commitment with a lot on the table.

However, it's all worth it when you see it succeed and can feel the impact of a vision coming to life.

Entrepreneurs are builders, and they have an instinctual trait that drives growth. I've met over a thousand business owners and heard the journeys of how they got started, what they do now, and how it all panned out both personally and financially. Through this experience, I noticed that the most financially successful entrepreneurs have a key commonality: they built the majority of their wealth through focus on one company.

They had a habit of continually re-investing in their business, avoiding side deals and distractions, and growing their core business to levels they had only dreamed of.

They understood their opportunity cost.

There are a lot of financially successful entrepreneurs that have built balance sheets of $5 million, $10 million, or even $20 million with lots of different investments and businesses. But the $50 million, $100 million, or even billion-dollar balance sheets were usually built through a concentrated focus on one thing.

This focus is a powerful force for an owner, which is why so many struggle after they sell their company and get overwhelmed with the optionality and complexity of being an investor versus a builder. This is one of the most dangerous places an entrepreneur can go and is usually filled with many learning experiences. I'll cover much more on that when we discuss the Exit Strategy in Chapter 8.

When you are building a business, making re-investment decisions, managing emotions, and filtering opportunities, it is critical to have a Balance Sheet Strategy to keep you focused.

A Balance Sheet Strategy is the overarching investment and re-investment strategy for your entire balance sheet. It identifies all of your investments, businesses, private equity, public equity, real estate, fixed income, or cash. And what your specific strategy encompasses. It is important because it allows you to holistically view assets, returns, risk, and opportunity cost.

Questions That a Balance Sheet Strategy™ Addresses

- How is my Total Balance Sheet™ invested?

- What is my return on my business stock?

- What is my return on all of my other assets?

- If I have excess capital, where should it go? To pay down debt? Re-invest in the company? Invest in the stock market or real estate?

- What is my risk exposure?

- With my current strategy, what does my balance sheet look like three, five, ten years from now?

- What other opportunities might make sense for me?

- How does this all tie in with my goals?

THE ENTREPRENEUR'S INVESTMENT OPPORTUNITY DIAGRAM™

The Entrepreneur's Investment Opportunity Diagram (IOD™) is a WISE concept and tool used to illustrate the investment opportunities and unique balance sheet of an entrepreneur. This breaks down how entrepreneurs think about opportunities and often make decisions, even when it happens subconsciously. You'll likely find that this is how you think naturally, but in illustrated form.

Balance Sheet Strategy™

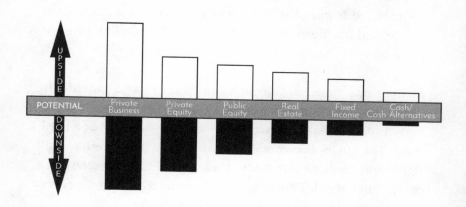

	Private Business	Private Equity	Public Equity	Real Estate	Fixed Income	Cash/ Cash Alternatives
Perceived Risk	LOW	HIGH	HIGH	LOW	LOW	LOW
Predictability	MEDIUM	LOW	MEDIUM	MEDIUM	HIGH	HIGH
Control	HIGH	MEDIUM	LOW	HIGH	LOW	LOW
Opportunity Cost	HIGH	MEDIUM	LOW	HIGH	LOW	LOW
Liquidity	LOW	LOW	HIGH	LOW	HIGH	HIGH
Pricing Accuracy	LOW	LOW	HIGH	LOW	HIGH	HIGH

The first component of the IOD is the entrepreneur's business. This usually has the highest potential upside. The entrepreneur created it. Their own unique talents and skillset contributed toward the business's success, and it could have a potential upside return of 20 percent, 50 percent, or even 1,000 percent.

At the same time, any single business also has a potentially unlimited downside. The business could go bankrupt. It could have no asset value. There could be an industry shift or a legal issue. The business owner could get hit by a bus. These are all significant, realistic downsides that we don't always take seriously—but should. This column represents what many owners say is their best and most important investment.

The second component of the Investment Opportunity Diagram is private equity. This involves investments in private companies, as an angel investor, through a fund, or directly in a venture that your friend might own. Such an investment could be completely nondiversified or diversified across a series of companies like a private equity fund.

This route also has substantial potential upside, and if diversified, could have some level of downside risk reduction vs. one company. Private equity investments are generally illiquid and involve a holding period of several years. In theory, if you had a large basket of diversified private companies, you should generate a stock-like return plus a liquidity premium—a fancy way of saying an extra return because your money is tied up for a period. This is all before you account for fees, expenses, or the time required to obtain the investments.

The third component of the Investment Opportunity Diagram is public equity. This is where you invest in the traditional stock markets, ideally in a diversified way. Over the long term, buying a portfolio or index of stocks has a substantially lower level of risk than your own business, but it also has a lower level of potential return.

There are many stock market indices, both domestic and international. To keep it simple, in my examples, I'll reference the most well-known index, the Standard & Poor's 500, or S&P 500,[2] which has averaged approximately 10 percent annual return since its inception. Assuming you're diversified and invest long-term, you can mitigate the downside risk of any individual company as well as the likelihood of loss of capital.

Next on the Investment Opportunity Diagram, we have investments in single-family real estate. Average home values over the past 80 years have increased approximately 5.5 percent.[3] A major difference is that real estate is a more tangible asset, which impacts the perception of risk. You can touch it, feel it, rent it—and there is a higher level of control and understanding, which results in making larger commitments of capital and even using leverage. It's usually a long-term investment that you are likely to hold in good times and bad. Furthermore, with leverage or debt, you can enhance returns, especially when interest rates are low.

---

2 You cannot invest directly in the index, however there are many investment instruments that can mimic the return of the index, minus fees.

3 Source: US Census Data/Millionacres.com.

Next we have fixed income, which is a fancy way of saying bonds. Bonds have been around for centuries and come in all shapes and sizes. To keep it simple, investing in bonds has historically generated a long-term return of approximately 3 to 6 percent, depending on credit quality and maturity (time period).

Finally, on the Investment Opportunity Diagram, there are cash and cash alternatives. This is money in the bank, certificates of deposit, US treasuries. Your safe money. The cash off the table. It generates a low return, but it's liquid and there when you need it.

Each item on the diagram has an expected return, a level of risk, a level of control, and an allocation of time. To accurately measure the rate of return you generate involves not just the gross returns you make but also the time invested, the associated expenses, and the tax impact. Over time, opportunity cost will play a huge role in your investment decisions—and the most successful entrepreneurs and investors have made major strides in understanding and applying opportunity cost.

THE ENTREPRENEUR'S OPPORTUNITY COST

We all know what opportunity cost is, but we don't necessarily factor it in when making investment decisions. We tend to focus on the outcome, which is simpler and often more fun. "I bought a piece of real estate for $1.6 million and sold it for $2.4 million three years later." Usually, with limited measurement of the hard and soft costs, personal time, and resources that were needed to generate that return.

Let's walk through some simple explanations of the way opportunity connects to your decisions, your business, and your Balance Sheet Strategy (even if you don't realize you already have one).

Opportunity cost is the loss of a potential gain from a higher-yielding investment when a lower-yielding investment is chosen. If you invested in an opportunity and earned a 2 percent return when you could have invested in something else and earned a 10 percent return, you had an 8 percent *opportunity cost* on that capital.

When calculating opportunity cost, you have to consider *all* costs. If you can save ten cents on a gallon of gasoline by driving for an extra twenty minutes to a gas station that has lower prices, you don't just weigh the cost per gallon of gas. You also have to look at the time invested in traveling to that other location, the additional gas that was consumed driving there, the number of gallons you're buying, and what you could have been doing during that twenty minutes you were driving. Examining opportunity cost allows you to see the full picture and make the best decision.

Let's consider an example of a lawyer who charges $500 an hour. If that lawyer were to spend two hours washing her car, in theory, she's losing $1,000 of income by doing an activity that could have been outsourced for $20 an hour. The opportunity cost is very high for her. In contrast, for someone who makes $15 an hour working in retail, it makes total sense to wash their car themselves because the opportunity cost is not high. It will actually save them money.

This is where many entrepreneurs end up taking bad advice from the wrong sources. They talk to a friend who may have a very different opportunity cost for their time. The friend might say, "Why would you pay a lawyer to draft your legal documents? I did it on LegalZoom and saved thousands of dollars versus what the lawyer charged."

On its face, this seems to make sense. But that particular individual may have a lot of free time and may not have to give up many resources to do that task. Meanwhile, the business owner whose time has a very high value would incur a huge opportunity cost to do that legal work on his own, not to mention the risk of making a mistake.

Using this same principle with your investment decisions can make a huge impact on the outcome.

The most successful entrepreneurs have mastered this mindset and calculation, many times primarily through instinct, and it may be the single most important component of every future decision they make in business, investments, and life.

Determining your opportunity cost requires considering the ways that you spend your time or money that will yield the highest overall return. Rather than looking at each opportunity in isolation, this method takes the full balance sheet into consideration so that you can choose the opportunities that generate the best outcome overall. If you are going to re-invest your hard-earned capital in something, make sure you know what you are getting and what you are giving up so that the capital is working for you the right way, consistent with your overall vision and focus.

The Investment Opportunity Diagram and the entrepreneur's opportunity cost can become tremendously impactful to every future decision you make on your investment strategy—especially when looking at the Re-investment Dilemma. By understanding and prioritizing return, risk, control, and opportunity cost, we can better plan, assess, and decide where to invest. We can also shift over time as our goals and appetite for risk change.

RE-INVESTMENT DECISIONS

Most business owners do not have a re-investment strategy for their balance sheet. If they have extra profit, it might sit in cash, get invested in real estate, an investment deal that they heard about from one of their friends, or in their securities portfolio. As we outlined earlier in the book, there is rarely a defined strategy. This creates a less than optimal outcome and leads to more challenges with the Re-investment Dilemma.

The first step in creating a re-investment strategy is to understand your Investment Opportunity Diagram. This starts with establishing a fair value for your company—and I don't mean an intense process of hiring a valuation firm to do a formal assessment of your business. This simply means identifying a relatively accurate value of what your company is worth today, if you were to sell it.

The vast majority of business owners do not track their enterprise value and the annual return on their stock relative to that value. They track their profit and loss, they might even say that their company is worth five times earnings, but they do not track the actual value and the associated annual return of their company.

Shocking, isn't it? We invest forty to seventy hours a week in building a company and don't track its true return.

An example of a clear enterprise value sounds something like this:

> The enterprise value of ABC, Inc., is $37,000,000. This is based on a 6× multiple of EBIDTA, accounting for cash, debt, and assuming fair market salaries for owners.

Say your three-year goal is to grow the enterprise value from $37 million to $50 million while distributing a $500,000 annual shareholder dividend. Your expected annual growth rate on your stock is approximately 10 percent with an annual dividend of approximately 1 percent for an approximate total annual return of 11 percent.

You might be saying to yourself, "Well, that isn't rocket science." And it isn't. But the reality is most owners simply do not do it. They don't track an accurate enterprise value, or the annual return on their company stock based on that enterprise value.

They usually don't have a Total Balance Sheet. In fact, I find that the majority of owners in the $10 million–$100 million net worth range know their assets off the top of their head, and they might have put together a net worth statement for the bank, but they rarely have a Total Balance Sheet with all of their assets and businesses at fair market value.

Why is knowing enterprise value important? Well, if your company was growing its enterprise value at 5 percent, and it was worth $37 million, you might prefer to sell the company and have lower risk and a higher expected return in another investment or business. Alternatively, if your company is growing at a much higher rate than other risk assets, you might want to re-invest more capital back in the business to capture that growth.

Think about it this way: you are making a conscious decision to hold a $37 million investment in ABC, Inc. If you are going to do that, you had better be incredibly clear about what that investment returns, as well as the opportunity cost of your alternatives.

Not establishing an enterprise value and annual return for your company creates a huge challenge in your re-investment decisions because you have no measurement of your largest asset.

Establishing an enterprise value and a rate of return will allow you to accurately compare the return of your company versus other investments, whether business, real estate, or the stock market. You'll have a clear picture of your assets so you can make the best decision.

Furthermore, there are qualitative and quantitative factors that will directly impact the multiple you might receive on your company, therefore significantly impacting your enterprise value. Quantitative factors include things like revenue, earnings, margins, operating expenses, etc. Qualitative factors include things like years in business, management tenor, specialization, brand awareness, customer loyalty, etc.

Business owners tend to focus on only the multiple of earnings to determine a value. Your industry average might be 6×, but based on these qualitative and quantitative factors, your company could be worth up to 8× or down to 4×.

Through reviewing these factors, you may realize that you have a lower margin than your peers, and investing in operational efficiency might create larger earnings resulting in a larger enterprise value. Knowing these items and planning for increased value can sometimes be your best investment and will directly impact your re-investment decision.

Once you have your enterprise value, you'll want to identify all the additional assets on your balance sheet and their returns. This includes brokerage accounts, businesses, IRAs, 401(k)s, real estate, private equity, insurance cash values, etc.

Your list could be four items or forty items, but you will need to have it all down with expected return assumptions for each. This can be an intense exercise, but necessary and worthwhile. In Chapter 11, I'll show you the process that brings this all together with a clear path.

With all of your assets laid out and their expected returns, you can holistically view your entire balance sheet and see how you are currently allocated and how you are performing and make better decisions on where to invest going forward.

Seeing the Total Balance Sheet with enterprise value and growth projections creates a lot more clarity on your position and will also identify major gaps and issues in your strategy. This perspective will allow you to set more intentional goals.

For re-investment decisions, the best path forward becomes clearer when all of your options are laid out and weighed against your goals—personal, business, and financial.

If you think about the options on the Investment Opportunity Diagram as tools on a tool belt, you might have only been using a screwdriver and a hammer up until now, as our natural tendency is to stick with what we know. But that often results in limitations and bottlenecks. With a deeper knowledge of what other tools can do and how they can give you leverage, you can change your outcome.

Implementing those tools requires knowing what you have, knowing your options, setting your goal, and creating the best combined strategy to get you there.

BALANCE SHEET STRATEGY™ IN ACTION

In 2014, a business owner named Alex came to me with the idea to invest in Houston's real estate market. He'd been paying six figures in rent and had decided that owning the building and creating equity would be a better investment than continuing to pay rent on the property.

I agreed with him that real estate is a great investment—and one of the best investments of all time. But that wasn't the question he was really asking. Under the surface, he needed to know whether real estate was the best investment opportunity *for him at that time.*

We reviewed the Investment Opportunity Diagram and looked at what his options were for a re-investment strategy. Looking at his balance sheet, Alex realized he could put that money in real estate, keep it in cash, or find an alternative place to invest.

What better place than his own company?

"I'm curious," I asked. "Since your company is still expanding, what would happen if you put that same capital in your company rather than toward buying this property? What would your return be?"

He hadn't thought of it that way at all, so we made it more tangible. Alex determined that if he were to invest the real estate capital back into the company through the hiring of new consultants, his return would be 30 to 40 percent.

On the other hand, his real estate investment had an expected return of about 15 percent.

With hiring consultants, his opportunity cost wouldn't be much because he already had the infrastructure in place to support those consultants. For the latter, he would have to contend with a new business in real estate. Among other considerations, he would need a property management company or to learn to run it himself.

Neither decision would be wrong, depending on what he really wanted.

With his options more clearly defined, his eyes lit up, and he knew his answer: "I don't want to be in a new business. I'll keep the return I can get here in my own business. And increased earnings on my business also increase my company value. The more earnings, the better my multiple if I sell."

Now, years down the road, Alex may be ready to make that property purchase. At some point, excess profit will reach a level where he can invest in his company *and* other opportunities, without having to choose. He may even be able to buy a bigger building with a better property management company and start up a second enterprise—but only if he wants to.

So what about the other components of the Investment Opportunity Diagram? We've talked about business and real estate, and most business owners instinctively understand these investments. But what about investment in stocks and bonds? Where do they fit in? Are there more tools that can leverage success?

The reality is that the most misunderstood investment for entrepreneurs is the stock market. Why? Because to be successful, it requires the opposite mindset to our natural instincts.

We control our business. We understand our business. We view our business long-term. We invest in our business long-term. We are patient with our business results. And we perceive the risk of our business as low.

In contrast, we cannot control the market. We usually don't understand the market. We view the market short-term. We usually invest in the market short-term. We are impatient with market performance. And we perceive the market as high risk.

If you look at the facts over the long term, the stock market, which I'll simplify to just the S&P 500, has delivered a 10 percent annual return, with a high level of diversification and long-term predictability.

If you told me I had to put a million dollars away for the next twenty years and I couldn't touch it or modify anything, the first investment I would pick would be in the S&P 500 index. Why? Because I would be investing in diversified entrepreneurship.

The index is a basket of the 500 largest and most widely traded companies in the most entrepreneurial country in the world. The companies in the basket get recycled, the bad performing companies get kicked out, and the best performing new companies get added, and over the long-term, this would constantly provide protection against disruption and industry transformation.

In 2000, my top five holdings would have been General Electric, Exxon Mobil, Pfizer, Citigroup, and Cisco. In 2010, they would be Exxon Mobil, Apple, Microsoft, Berkshire Hathaway, and General Electric. And in 2020, they would have been Apple, Microsoft, Amazon, Facebook, and Google. Over that twenty years, companies like Enron and Lehman Brothers would get pushed out as companies like Google, Amazon, and Tesla get added.

The index is perceived as static, but in reality, it is quite dynamic.

Historically speaking, the S&P 500 has delivered a 10 percent return, triple the rate of inflation, five times the rate of savings or CDs, and with a limited investment of time. Providing a powerful passive investment strategy.

Warren Buffett, arguably the most successful investor in history, advises his followers as well as his children to buy the certainty of the market index. His success in investing has many reasons, but one very large reason is staying unemotional when crises arise and always knowing that, underneath all the media noise, the market represents a group of the most successful companies in the world, and they are constantly innovating and reinventing themselves.

The future is incredibly uncertain, but if you believe that entrepreneurship will always innovate a new solution, investing in the market index might be the most relevant investment outside of your own business.

The point of investing capital is to make a return and outpace the rate of inflation over time. If we assume average long-term inflation at 2–3 percent, you can earn potentially double that rate in a long-term bond portfolio, double to triple that rate in real estate, and triple to quadruple that rate in stocks and unlock a universe of potential outcomes in your own business.

WISE is not an investment strategy, nor does it prescribe one investment over another. You can build a Balance Sheet Strategy using any combination of investments, but it is important to know the facts and reality of our options, not just our perceptions.

At the end of the day, you have to feel comfortable with whatever path you take. Whether it's 100 percent in one company until you exit or a combination of several.

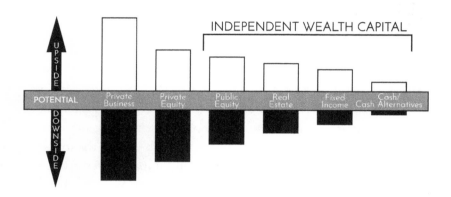

There are two sides to the Investment Opportunity Diagram. The left side represents your investment in business and private equity. These two columns generally have higher risk, higher expected return, and less predictability. And the right side includes investments in the market, real estate, bonds, and cash. Generally, these four columns are more predictable and diversified. Capital you and your family can depend on over the long-term.

Over time, you can take profits from the left side and capture them on the right side. The formula will depend on your goals, but generally speaking, most business owners want to establish enough on the right side to have Independent Wealth™ (financial independence). Thus giving them further freedom to take risks in business or simply have independence and financial security.

CHAPTER 6

LIQUIDITY & CASH FLOW™

*Divide Your Capital to Create
a Better Outcome*

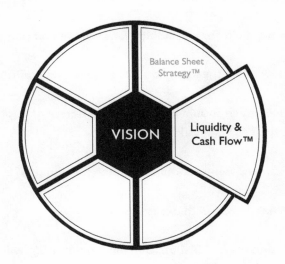

LIQUIDITY & CASH FLOW IS THE WAY YOU POSITION, DISTRIBUTE, manage, and use all of your cash. It includes your working capital in the company; your salary, bonus, distributions, and all of your savings; and your passive income streams, both business and personal. This is important because everything starts and ends with cash flow.

The issue is that most entrepreneurs view their cash as one lump sum of capital and do not divide it based on goals. This leads to significant inefficiencies and lost purchasing power over time.

Liquidity & Cash Flow addresses questions like:

- What are all my sources of income and cash flow, both from my company and all other investments?

- How much capital should I leave in the company?

- How much personal liquidity should I maintain?

- How much should I maintain for a potential opportunity or as a rainy-day fund?

- How and where should I position my liquidity?

- What do I do with excess liquidity?

Addressing these questions and having a strategy will result in greater financial efficiency, better debt management, better return on cash, increased or decreased liquidity based on goals, and ensuring that excess capital is working harder for you.

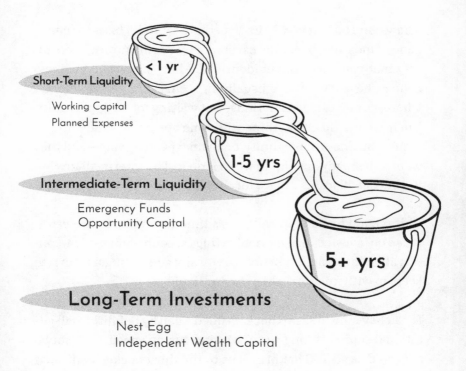

Short-Term Liquidity

Working Capital
Planned Expenses

Intermediate-Term Liquidity

Emergency Funds
Opportunity Capital

Long-Term Investments

Nest Egg
Independent Wealth Capital

LIQUIDITY BUCKETS™

The first bucket is working capital. This refers to how much cash you need to run your company. It's how much liquid cash you will need in order to effectively replenish inventory, pay employees and vendors, handle the ups and downs of expenses, and make sure that you have ample cash on hand to run the company. This first bucket has a timeline of less than twelve months. The funds are usually in a checking or operating account earning little to no return.

The second bucket is your intermediate capital. This is for emergency funds and/or capital earmarked for some future opportunity that you have not yet identified. Many successful business owners have cash that's usually in a checking account somewhere, not invested in anything, just waiting for an opportunity. Their logic is that something will come up—a real estate investment, a business opportunity, or an unexpected event—and they want to be ready and liquid when it does. The intermediate capital bucket allocates a place for these funds.

This second bucket typically has a timeline of one to five years. It can be invested in high-yield savings accounts or an ultra-conservative investment portfolio, typically generating a return to keep up with inflation while staying liquid.

If you have the first two buckets filled, then by definition, all additional capital is long-term, with no current need, and can be allocated as such. That brings us to the third bucket, dedicated to a long-term investment strategy. This investment strategy is based on what you built in your Balance Sheet Strategy. If you have extra liquidity, you now have a clear path to re-invest it.

After liquidity, there's the cash flow component to consider. This is all the money that's coming in from your company, as well as your different investments in the form of cash flow. How do you apply that cash, and what do you do with the excess? If you need 50 percent of your capital to go back into your company for re-investment, that's great—but what's happening with the other 50 percent? Is it going to be applied to paying off your mortgage, paying down company loans, or re-investing in real estate or the stock market? What is the best way to allocate the money?

Time is money. Having a Balance Sheet Strategy and Liquidity Buckets puts a framework around your capital so you can direct it quickly and efficiently to the appropriate place. **With this method, you don't have to rethink what to do every time a lump sum of cash comes in.** There's a predetermined strategy that you thought about during a strategic planning session versus reacting in the moment to whatever happens with cash flow. Without a plan, that cash is usually spent, put into something that wasn't well thought out, or just parked in a bank account, eroding to inflation.

Intentional, integrated planning reveals all kinds of issues that business owners never even knew they had, and situations like this are more common than you might think. So many business owners have their focus on company growth that it's hard for them to move away from that and examine the bigger picture.

Because of their success, their personal wealth has become a business of its own.

LIQUIDITY & CASH FLOW™ IN ACTION

Several years ago, Max was introduced to me by his CPA. But almost immediately, he said, "I'm not sure why I was referred to you. *I'm all set.* I have two tax advisors, I have a legal advisor, two financial advisors, an insurance agent, a captive insurance company, trusts, and partnerships. I don't know what in the world could be set up that I don't already have established. I'm just coming to meet with you because my CPA recommended it. I really think I've got things in good order."

Within WISE, one of the exercises we did with Max was to build out a Total Balance Sheet of all of his various companies' cash positions in addition to those of his partnerships, trusts, and personal investments. Using the Liquidity & Cash Flow tools and processes, we concluded that he needed $3 million of total liquidity to meet his objectives—$1 million in working capital (Bucket 1) and $2 million for an upcoming business expansion he was planning (Bucket 2). Anything above that amount could be allocated to his long-term investment strategy (Bucket 3).

I started by asking Max, "How much liquidity do you think you have between all of your different investments, cash accounts, and entities?"

Max made an educated guess as to how much and said, "Likely around $3 million."

I pulled out a report of his Total Balance Sheet with all his cash and assets integrated together, and we discovered he actually had close to $7 million sitting in cash. This was at the end of 2013, where cash in the bank earned zero return, and equity markets were up around 30 percent for the year. At the time, Max's long-term portfolio investments were allocated 50 percent to stocks and 50 percent to bonds.

Essentially, had that $4 million in excess cash been invested, it could have returned around $600,000 in that year alone—his opportunity cost for poor cash management topped half a million.

The interesting part of this story is that Max was largely unaware that his cash position was that large, and he certainly had no idea how much that unawareness cost him. I still remember the expression on his face when he saw the numbers: shock, disappointment, curiosity, and urgency, all at the same time.

While Max knew he had plans in place, he was missing the system and process to bring all the pieces together.

WISE doesn't let intention slip. By identifying what you want, then overlaying that against every item on your balance sheet, you form a roadmap and decision model to capture and maximize your success.

CHAPTER 7

LIFESTYLE & LEGACY™

*Compartmentalize Your Assets Based on
What's for You and What's for Your Legacy*

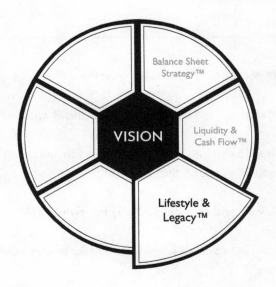

Do you ever ask yourself why? Why did I build all of this? Why do I continue to build it? Is it for fun? For my children? For me?

There are two distinct sides to your wealth. What's for you—that's Lifestyle. And what's for someone else—that's Legacy. What you do with each of these is your choice—well, you *and* your spouse.

All of the capital you have on your balance sheet can be specifically allocated to a certain goal. Is this Lifestyle Capital—spending, investing in deals, living, and enjoying? Or is this Legacy Capital—your children, your beneficiaries, or your charitable intentions? This step is important because it defines the specific goal for each part of your wealth, which will directly impact how you view and position it.

Lifestyle & Legacy™ addresses questions like:

- How much do I need for financial independence?

- How do I ensure I have capital for fun, investing in deals, and taking risks?

- How should I position money for my heirs?

- How do I address empowerment vs. entitlement of my heirs?

- How can I integrate my goals for legacy to minimize tax?

- How do I create financial continuity for my spouse and family?

- How do I maximize the value of all that I have built?

LIFESTYLE VS. LEGACY

For years, you have been building and building, and subconsciously you have a reason why—whether that is for security, freedom, habit, or just for fun. However, with all your success, you might have reached a point where what you have is more than you will ever need. Essentially, the current assets you have are more than enough to provide for the desired lifestyle you want. Resulting in excess wealth that you will likely never use or spend yourself.

If you know what is truly excess, you can plan for that excess differently than you might plan otherwise. And that freedom can create new opportunities.

With that level of success also comes new challenges of managing it.

You may be wondering whether you should involve your children in the business or give equity to them if they are already involved. You may be debating whether you should establish a trust or an estate plan or some type of succession mechanism. You might even be debating giving them a lump sum of money using the estate tax exemption that your CPA or attorney has been mentioning as an opportunity.

Your wealth may even be significant enough that you're wondering whether you should establish a family office or some type of entity to manage all of the wealth you've built.

Organizing all of these thoughts and opportunities is very challenging and can be quite paralyzing. In many cases, I see estate plans being worked on for years and years with no real action. Or something being established but with limited vision and management to a clear strategy. In some cases, I've seen lots of really expensive documents in place, but with no actual assets being transferred.

These are all surface issues of the Legacy Dilemma. The core questions that need to be answered are these: What capital do I need to live the lifestyle that I want? And what capital is excess that I can allocate for my legacy?

Understanding the kind of lifestyle you want now and the legacy you want to live and/or leave is the key. **Your wealth has to be assessed based on what *you* want to do with it.**

The Lifestyle & Legacy concept illustrates these areas in simple form.

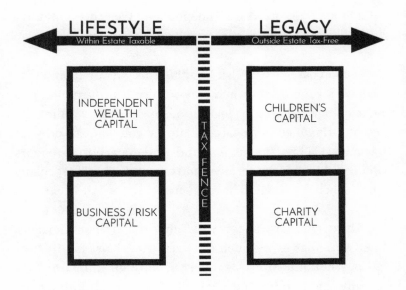

Referencing the diagram, there are four categories representing the different aspects of Lifestyle & Legacy Capital. The first category is Independent Wealth Capital. That's how much capital you need to establish separate from your company to meet your long-term needs and desires for income. I've found that most owners want to establish capital separate from the company so that, over time, they have complete financial independence.

Generally, this capital is invested in more predictable assets that generate income such as stocks, bonds, or real estate. This is predictable capital. You can position this Independent Wealth Capital in a way that you are confident will provide income security.

The amount you need for Independent Wealth Capital answers the part of the big question: how much is enough?

The second category is Risk Capital—this is your capital that you have for fun, growth, and opportunity. It is the money you can take high risks with, whether business risks or rolling the dice on private equity deals—whatever you want to do with that capital is fine. It's the *fun* fund. And many entrepreneurs will need this to feel free, alive, and engaged. This is especially true for those who sell their core business.

The third category is for your children or beneficiaries. When you hear terms such as "trust funds" or "family limited partnership interests," it is usually an indicator that someone has established a vehicle for their children. This category is often tied to lots of emotion around empowerment or entitlement.

The fourth category is Charity, if you're so inclined. This is capital that you give or allocate to a charitable purpose. If you are charitable, there are substantial tax benefits in this category, and we will discuss some of these considerations later in the book.

The left side of the chart represents what's in your name, what's part of your estate, and what's subject to estate tax. The right side is what is moved outside your estate, is no longer in your name, and is potentially free of estate tax. This impacts things substantially, as the current estate tax rate in the United States is 40 percent (as of 2021).

We will discuss this further when we get to Lifetime Tax Strategy in Chapter 10. **For now, what is important to remember is for all the money you leave behind, there are only three places it can go: family, charity, or government.** If you plan right, you can help ensure that what you have built can go the place you desire, which is usually a combination of the first two.

LIFESTYLE & LEGACY™ IN ACTION

Mark had built a highly successful manufacturing company over the course of thirty years. His wife, Cindy, was somewhat involved in the business, but her true passion was real estate. And Cindy had built a substantial real estate business as well, investing in retail and commercial buildings. They had four children, with one of them, Rebecca, being heavily involved in the manufacturing business.

Mark led the external side of the company, customers, and strategic partners. He had a gift for relationship building and getting deals done. Rebecca, his daughter, led the operations, infrastructure, and employees of the company. Rebecca started working for the company when she was in college and had worked there full-time for fifteen years. She knew the business inside and out, had the trust of the employees, and was her dad's clear second in command. Her official title was COO.

Mark and Cindy had a will and an estate plan, and it was clearly laid out. If something were to happen to either Mark or Cindy, all of their assets would go to each other. If something happened to both of them, all the assets would be split between their four children, with 10 percent going to charity.

Sounds pretty straightforward, right?

I asked Mark, "If you weren't around, who would you want to run the business?" Mark answered almost instantaneously, "Rebecca—she already runs the business. I have total trust she will do a great job."

I looked over at Cindy. She agreed and said, "Rebecca is a huge part of the success of the company and has aspirations to take over one day."

They both had tremendous confidence in Rebecca. But there were several issues. Under the current plan, Cindy would have ownership and control of a company that she doesn't want to run, four siblings would eventually have joint control of a company that three are not involved in, and the one child who has enhanced the success of the business and has the skills and inclination to run it has no control of anything. And there was still much more to this iceberg of complications.

I brought these considerations to Mark and Cindy, and at first glance, they were inclined to think all would be fine. The kids all get along, and Rebecca would surely have the trust of her siblings. After all, they have watched her build the company with Dad for over a decade.

After a second look, and more discussion on the potential family conflict issues, they felt different. The business was worth over $30 million and growing substantially, and it needed to have a more intentional plan.

Mark and Cindy wanted to be fair to their children, but fair didn't necessarily mean equal. And Cindy didn't want to be a barrier to Rebecca's growth of the company. **They both wanted the success of the company to benefit all of the children, but they didn't want to create a catalyst for conflict between the children.** They also did not want to be financially dependent on the business for income, especially if Mark were not around.

To get more clarity, we went back to the WISE tool for Lifestyle & Legacy Capital. First, we identified how much Mark and Cindy needed to fulfill their wants, needs, and desires and earmarked that money as Independent Wealth Capital. The Independent Wealth Capital was filled with real estate and their portfolios of stocks and bonds.

We identified that they needed $20 million in Independent Wealth Capital to meet their income goals. Between the real estate and their portfolios, they had around $15 million, and we built a plan to fill the gap through saving future distributions from the company.

We then identified how much of the company ownership Mark wanted to maintain for future growth participation. That amount was 60 percent of the company shares.

Now that they had a clear view of what they both wanted for their *Lifestyle Capital*, we could more effectively assess what they wanted for their *Legacy Capital*.

It was clear that the company was to be run by Rebecca, but they didn't want the other children to be excluded. They established a trust for Rebecca and sold 40 percent of their shares to the trust, which Rebecca planned to pay back from the future income of the shares. The payments would be used to help fill the $5 million gap that Mark and Cindy needed to reach $20 million of Independent Wealth Capital. The excess would be additional capital that they could spend or give away.

All of the children would eventually receive shares in the company, but they would be nonvoting shares, with an option to sell at fair value. This way, if the children wanted to be silent partners, they could, but if they wanted to cash out, they had that option as well.

A board was to be established to ensure checks and balances. Rebecca would have a fair market compensation package for her employment. A baseline formula would be established to determine a percentage of profits that could be distributed annually, creating an income stream for all shareholders. The first chairman of the board would be Mark; this way, he could oversee the process and ensure things were running as intended. And hopefully for a long time.

Under this formula, even if Mark and Cindy lived to be one hundred, they would have all the Independent Wealth Capital required to meet their needs as well as control of the company. If Mark were to pass, Rebecca would take management control of the shares (even if she didn't have 51 percent), and Cindy and the children could receive dividends and profits. Cindy would have her financial independence. And most importantly, the children could minimize conflict. If they wanted to be partners, they could. If not, they could sell their shares and have more cash. And the charitable goals were to be met through liquid assets as opposed to company shares, keeping the complexity lower and establishing a family charity fund that all the children and grandchildren could participate in.

Using the framework and thinking of Lifestyle & Legacy Capital entirely changed the outcome of their estate, succession, and cash flow strategy. It gave Mark and Cindy the ability to separate and compartmentalize the assets based on what they were for. **By focusing on the end goal, the decisions changed.**

It created a simple solution for a complex problem.

There were a lot of details to this plan that had to be worked out, and the tax and legal planning created lots of efficiencies. But the big picture fundamentals were led by Lifestyle vs. Legacy Capital—in this case, "Who runs the company?"

This story shed light on the key questions you need to address for what you want for you vs. what you want for your legacy. It's much easier to think about what you want to leave as a legacy once you know that you have enough for yourself.

When we discuss business succession planning in the upcoming chapter, you'll learn that the most successful company succession plans are executed over many years and how critical it is that you identify a leadership model and successor for the next generation.

CHAPTER 8

EXIT STRATEGY

Operating with the End in Mind

DO YOU EVER THINK ABOUT SELLING YOUR COMPANY? PASSING
it to your children? Selling it to your management team or employees? Many owners build their company with the aspiration
of one day selling it for an eight-, nine-, or ten-figure sum. Oth-

ers can't even imagine selling their company. It's their identity, their purpose, their passion, and their source of income and wealth.

Regardless of your mindset toward an exit, there are three eventual paths you can take with your company. The Exit Strategy addresses all three: exit, succession, and continuity. Exit through a sale of your company to a third party. Succession of your company to a family member or management team. Continuity of your company in the event of the unexpected.

The Exit Strategy is important as your business is the largest asset on your balance sheet and highly connected to you.

Philosophically, a business owner should always be thinking about their exit.

Sometimes it will happen as planned, and sometimes it will happen unexpectedly—but no business can be kept forever. You will exit, whether voluntary or involuntary, and it's important to be proactive about it. Setting your business up now for an effective transfer and making a plan for what might happen after you're no longer running it will make that transition better for everyone involved.

If you're feeling stress rising up around locking an exit plan in place, breathe a sigh of relief: you don't have to permanently commit to the plan you make. It can change. The steps to plan for exit, succession, and continuity are very similar. A business that can be effectively transitioned is a business that's running well, and that's good for every goal.

The Exit Strategy address questions like:

- What is my end goal for the business?

- How do I maximize the value of my company if and when I sell?

- What is the difference between the Enterprise Value of my company and the net proceeds I would receive if I sold?

- Should I sell to a third party? Pass to my child? Sell to management?

- What happens if I get hit by a bus?

- What needs to be in place to ensure the business can succeed?

- Will my team and family have what they need?

EXIT

If your plan is to sell your company to an external buyer, there is a lot to prepare for. When should you start preparing? Now. Even if you plan to sell in fifteen years, knowing what a buyer is looking for, knowing what to avoid, and knowing the exit process will enhance the value of your business.

For the owner who says, "I'm not *planning* to sell the company, but at the right price, anything's for sale," the question is this:

What are you doing today that is enhancing the value of your company so that when that offer arrives, it's as high as it can be?

In the chapter on Balance Sheet Strategy, we noted that there are quantitative and qualitative factors that drive the value of your business, or enterprise value. Quantitative factors include things like revenue, earnings, margins, operating expenses, etc. Qualitative factors include things like years in business, management tenor, specialization, brand awareness, customer loyalty, etc.

To maximize the value of your company, you'll want to know the factors that are important to a potential buyer, the strengths and weaknesses of your company, and your plan to drive value. This will help to ensure that, when and if you sell, it's at the right price.

You'll also want to know how much is enough so that once you sell your company, you have the capital you want for both your lifestyle and your legacy.

Succession

If you plan to pass your shares to your son or daughter, or to another internal party, there is also a lot to prepare for. The majority of family businesses will not make it through the second generation—70 to 80 percent will fail, depending on the statistics you pull. These failures come from a combination of factors, including poor succession planning, a lack of clear and direct control for the successor, and a successor who is not qualified to run the business.

If you're going to transfer your business to your children, it's important that they demonstrate some kind of success elsewhere before stepping in to take over. If they are placed in a leadership position, they need to be granted control over their department or domain and held accountable for their results, just as you would for a nonfamily team member.

For successful company succession, you must establish a single leader. Control can't be shared among multiple people—a business needs a clear leader.

Always remember, succession is a process, not an event. There is no document or moment that will make succession happen. It is a process that should be undertaken with intention and thoughtfulness from beginning to end.

Continuity

Continuity plans ensure the business can continue operating in the event of an unforeseen circumstance. At the time of this writing, we're in the midst of a global pandemic that has shut down many businesses and changed the path for countless others. Those who created a virtual continuity plan and had emergency cash reserves fared much better than those who did not.

Creating continuity for your business is critical. For most companies, the largest dependency is on the owner. If they were to be incapacitated or disabled, or pass away, what's the plan for continuity? How much capital would be needed? Who takes over control?

These plans will vary from business to business, so it's important to think through the potential challenges *your* company could face, identifying your gaps in planning and finding the effective solutions to fill them. Sometimes, just verbalizing what you want creates immense progress. Your advisors, team, and family have likely thought about these risks, and if you tell them your goal, they will want to help you support it.

Cross-Preparation

Each of the three paths is connected, and preparing for one helps you to be prepared for the other. Whether you sell the business to someone new or pass it along to someone you trust, a continuity plan will ensure success during that transfer. Whether you're expecting to sell soon and move on to a new adventure or you're building something that your heirs will operate, creating a business that can operate smoothly without you will help ensure continuity when that transition happens.

One operating model that I regularly recommend is EOS®, or the Entrepreneurial Operating System. I have used it in my own company, and many of my clients have used it in theirs. It's an operating system created by Gino Wickman, outlined in his book *Traction*, that helps entrepreneurial companies run more effectively and helps owners get what they want out of their business.

One of the exercises in EOS is creating an accountability chart. This involves separating major functions of the business into different accountabilities rather than separating it by people.

Often, we see that the business is viewed as *dad* and *brother* and *sister*, rather than the specific roles and responsibilities they fulfill. Dad might be doing functions that are in five different job descriptions because he's been there for thirty years, and that's the way it's been. Brother handles sales and marketing. Sister does operations and human resources and also some sales.

This creates an issue because you can't replace Dad.

But, by dividing the functions needed for the business and creating an accountability chart, you can separate the people from the function. So if Dad is no longer around, we know the functions that Dad fulfilled and can have someone else in the company or outside of it take over those specific functions. This process increases clarity, which helps create a better outcome.

Implementing a system like EOS years in advance allows for a much higher likelihood of succession than if you wait for the family member to pass away or step into an exit suddenly without a plan. I also believe that a system like EOS increases alignment within the organization, and that can drive the overall value higher.

EXIT STRATEGY IN ACTION

For one owner, the answer was apparently easy. James spent thirty years building his company. It was his life's work, and his plan was to pass it along to his son, Luke.

"Great, does Luke know that?"

He skirted around the question for a minute, then admitted that there was no real plan in place. They'd discussed it briefly, but it hadn't gone any further. What's more, when he finally asked Luke directly, he was very hesitant. He liked the idea but didn't know if it was his path.

James was beginning the WISE journey and addressing all six of the planning components. I expressed to James that succession is a process and not an event and encouraged him to involve Luke in his strategic planning sessions so Luke could have the exposure to see if it is something he desires.

"It will also give you more clarity as to whether Luke has what it takes to run the company," I explained.

After spending a year working together on the strategic side of the business, Luke decided that he didn't want to be CEO at all because after watching what Dad did, he wasn't interested in that kind of work. Marketing was his sweet spot.

With the original "plans" off the table, James began to focus on maximizing value for a potential sale, not because he wanted to sell the company, but because he understood that planning for value enhancement is good practice in general. We began assessing the quantitative and qualitative aspects of the business and had talks with investment bankers to get a pulse on the market and further understand what his potential buyers valued. We found ways to re-invest James's profit to create more value for his business and use the excess to create optimal value for his personal balance sheet.

James used EOS, the Entrepreneurial Operating System, to organize his executive teams and systems and further step himself out of the day-to-day operations and make the business more viable for sale. He and his team created clear processes for all of the roles and responsibilities within the organization.

It took about three years to really get into stride on his new value enhancement and operational enhancement processes. Over this period, James had a big change in his mindset toward his business and became more focused than ever before. This focus on an end outcome created many benefits for James, both financially and mentally, as there was a clear path and plan.

His Balance Sheet Strategy involved taking a certain percentage of profits out of the company each year and re-investing them in his portfolio so he and his wife could have Independent Wealth—financial independence separate from the company. And the progress was incredible.

The company was growing faster than ever, and James had news to share. "I've recently been meeting with my son to discuss his future path in the company, and now that we have good infrastructure in place, he can more clearly see the whole business, and he wants to take over."

"I'm looking to simplify my role within the business and spend more time pursuing other interests. I am happy to tell you that we are moving forward with Luke as President of the company."

WISE created clarity for James on what he had and the options it provided. Knowing he had Independent Wealth separate from the company made him more comfortable letting go. Building a plan for Lifestyle & Legacy gave him clarity as to how he wanted to spend his time. Using the Entrepreneurial Operating System to run his company gave him and his son a shared vision on the whole business and got James out of the day-to-day responsibilities.

Increased perspective changed his outcome.

Starting the conversation with James about what he wanted for his Exit Strategy began a five-year journey to a much more successful outcome. The plan and outcome were unique to his situation and goals. It integrated the personal, business, and financial components of his life. And even though the plan changed along the way, the important thing was that he had an intentional plan in place.

SELLING YOUR COMPANY

An interesting statistic that has stuck with me for years relates to the dangers of mountain climbing. I learned that 80 percent of the accidents that happen when climbing mountains don't happen on the way up—they happen on the way down! People meticulously plan each step and stretch of effort required to get to the summit but overlook the journey back to safety.

If you think about the goal of most entrepreneurs, it might sound something like this: "my goal is to build this company and sell it for $100 million." Similarly, if someone talks about conquering Mount Everest, they talk about the dream of reaching the summit. But the reality is, **the true goal is reaching the summit and making it back down safely to celebrate and enjoy the accomplishment.** Statistics tell us the overlooked part is the latter.

In business succession, 80 percent of companies won't make it through the second generation. The vast majority of business owners will not monetize their company, let alone do it near their peak. And perhaps most shockingly, many of the owners that do sell their company at the top have a very hard time adjusting to the life after.

A PricewaterhouseCoopers study found that twelve months after selling, three out of four business owners profoundly regretted their decision.

There are several potential reasons for this, and we will explore them in the stories of Allan and Edward.

Allan had the type of climb and exit that people tell stories about. He was a European immigrant that started his software company with $500 and twenty-five years later had turned it into $500 million. He was in the software business before software was cool and lasted long after the dot-com boom and bust. Everyone who knew him or knew his story was enamored with his success and wanted to learn how he built such a great company.

To add to the story, Allan sold his company in 2007, right *before* the economic collapse. In hindsight, it may have been the perfect exit.

I met Allan about two years after the sale—we had been in touch for a while but were never able to actually connect as he was busy with the company, the exit, and everything that followed. I asked him how he built the company, and he lit up with joy talking me through the story of its beginning and the key milestones to its success.

Then I asked him his reason for selling the company. His facial expression changed, the joy moved toward logic, the excitement toward practicality, and he said, "It made sense to[long pause] I took the company as far as it could go, and it made sense to sell to a strategic buyer that could take it to the next level. It was good timing."

"Great," I said. "What a journey, and congratulations on your success. So what are you doing now?"

He went on to tell me about how he was involved in many different ventures. He started listing out all the deals. Real estate, private equity, family member investments, a restaurant, a racehorse, and considering setting up a family office or investment company to buy into software companies.

"Wow, that's a lot of things. All of this in just the past two years?" Allan laughed. He said, "I never understood why professional athletes went broke until I sold my company. **When you can say yes to almost anything, it's easy to lose control of your time and your money.** I'm spread so thin, invested in things I don't understand, and constantly feel like I am being pulled in every direction.

"Even my wife wants me to do things that I have never done before. It's like everyone knows since you aren't running your company, you have availability to do anything or invest in anything. It's the most overwhelming process I've ever experienced."

I wanted to say something, but I paused and just listened.

Allan went on, "When I started my company, I had a passion to build something. I had unlimited energy, all attached to a clear goal. Every step of the journey was with a clear goal. We scaled the company with a clear goal, we invested everything we had in the company, I had no distractions, no outside investments, everything was laser-focused on the company. Then, when I sold, everything changed. I lost my general, my troops, my artillery.

It's like the happiest day of my life was when I sold the company and the saddest day of my life was the day after, when I realized all that I lost. It sounds crazy, but that's how I feel sometimes."

I empathized and went on to tell Allan about the mountain climbing example. After hearing the story, he said, "Yes, that's me. I made it to the summit, and that was my goal, and now I'm really high up, the air is thin, and it's hard to breathe. I feel like I can go in any direction but can't climb any higher."

"Do you know what you want?" I asked. "Yes," Allan said. "I want to keep climbing."

Allan was in a tailspin. Where entrepreneurs feel like they've lost control of their life. Their purpose has gone. They're being pulled in different directions. Emotionally and mentally, they're struggling.

Without a clear path forward, all of that joy Allan felt right after selling began to dissipate. He had no idea who he was anymore or what he was meant to do. Where before he could create a vision, then suddenly see force applied to it to make it happen, now his visions were just on paper without anyone to channel it to. He was slipping and falling down the mountain, without any safety harness to catch him.

This happens quite often after selling a company. All of a sudden, the entrepreneur has two dozen investments and the most complicated balance sheet of their life, filled with all sorts of illiquid assets and no structure.

And with no company to run, the entrepreneur has no boundaries, which can lead to time quickly being tied up in things like mentoring businesses and overseeing investments. They can say yes to all these different things, and without clarity on what they *want* to say yes to, they can end up taking it all on.

In my experience, there's nothing more dangerous than a bored entrepreneur, and nothing more powerful than a focused one. Both can be especially true when you have lots of capital to deploy.

Part of the tailspin is situational, and you simply can't avoid it. Other parts can be planned for and managed. Overall, the transition is a challenging stage of the entrepreneurial journey, and some get trapped in it forever, never finding their footing.

Being intentional about what you want your life to look like after you sell the company—not just vague thoughts about the time you'll have or the money you'll get, but really making a plan—creates a different story altogether.

THE INTENTIONAL EXIT

Edward had been building his company for years. It had great cash flow and earnings. He had also built a nice nest egg from all the years of profits. He had good investments outside of his business as well as in his business. To put it simply, Edward was really successful and really comfortable.

I was having a meeting with Edward, or Ed, as he prefers to be called, and he was telling me about how the earnings multiples in his industry had really skyrocketed. He was considering whether it made sense to sell the company.

Ed had been using WISE for several years, and we referenced his blueprint to gain more perspective on his decision points. Based on all the numbers connected to his Lifestyle & Legacy goals, Ed had hit the Point of Optionality™. That's the point when what you have built is worth more than what you will never need.

Essentially, based on the goals Ed had for his Lifestyle & Legacy, if he were to sell his company, he would have enough capital to check all the boxes. Giving him the freedom to pursue whatever he desired with no concerns of downside.

Ed had a huge smile on his face. The excitement of having reached the summit was all-encompassing. He started asking "what about" questions—the ones that pop up when someone is questioning if everything has been thought about. What about longevity? What about charity? What about the economy? What about inflation?

Knowing Ed's situation and blueprint, I asked him, "Do you know what the most important 'what about' question is?"

His curiosity piqued.

"What about *what's next*?"

Ed had spent the prior years doing lots of good planning. Through WISE, he had clarity on cash flow, investment strategy, lifestyle goals, and legacy intentions—and he had established strategies to maximize his value and minimize his tax, if he ever sold.

But what we really needed to address at this life intersection was what came *next*. What was next for Ed and for the proceeds of his company. Two very critical decisions.

"Before we pull the trigger, we need to know what we will do after," I told Ed. "**Time and money are two very valuable assets, and selling your company would create a large influx of both.** Being intentional with what's next could be the most important decision you make."

Ed agreed, and we began our "what's next" conversations.

First, we talked through the reasons why he would sell. As you might imagine, it was more than just high multiples. Sometimes high multiples can be an enticing reason to consider an exit, but for most established and successful entrepreneurs, there needs to be more of a reason to sell than just money. This is their life's work, and they aren't just going to easily say goodbye.

Ed had two sides to his business—the service side and the product side. The service side generated a lot of cash, had a great reputation, and had brought the business to its current success. The product side was full of potential with opportunities to innovate, grow, and, most importantly, scale. Ed was excited about the product side, and although he loved the service side, it just didn't have the same potential.

We went through an exercise on creating your ideal life experience. One question I asked him was, "If you could wave your magic wand and have whatever allocation of time you desired, what would it look like?"

Ed said that he would love to work twenty to thirty hours per week on product development. Innovating, designing, and creating new things. This was connected to Ed's core enjoyment and passion. He loved to create. We used a WISE time mapping tool to allocate his time, starting with 365 days per year and allocating each and every day to whatever he desired. Innovating, travel, community work, sailing, and dedicated family time were all laid out, and at the end of the process, we had a map of Ed's dream life.

The second aspect of the decision was his wealth. What would Ed do with the capital, and what was his opportunity cost? So we reviewed the IOD (Investment Opportunity Diagram).

Based on our previous assumptions, Ed's company was worth around $20 million if he were to sell it. It made $3 million of profit each year, and revenue growth was relatively flat. Multiples had held steady around 7× earnings.

In the past, this had created a 15 percent cash flow for Ed ($3 million of cash flow on $20 million of company value), and considering he loved his work and knew the business, he was happy to continue building the company and saving profits. However, the market had strengthened, and his investment banker advised him that a 10–12× multiple was likely if he sold then.

Using the middle number of 11× earnings to run the math, the company was worth $33 million. A substantial increase from the $20 million currently on his balance sheet. Based on this potential valuation, the actual cash flow Ed would be receiving if he held the stock would be less than 10 percent. Based on the new market value, Ed was making $3 million of profit on a $33 million asset.

As we reviewed the numbers, Ed commented, "So, the way I see it, I used to make 15 percent on my stock. Based on the current market value, I would be making around 10 percent if I held it. So my decision is whether I want to hold the stock, keep all the risk, and hopefully make 10 percent, or sell, diversify and maybe make 6–8 percent in my investment portfolio and real estate, but with less risk."

I answered, "Yes, that's the return-on-investment decision."

"And the other decision?" Ed asked.

"Well, the other decision is the Return on Your Life Experience."

Ed had a moment of clarity: "Ideally, I would like to sell the company, but only if I could continue to build the product side as a new business. In that scenario, I get both the capital *and* the purpose." Ed had clarity that he had enough cash flow for his lifestyle and knew that his ideal allocation of time was innovating and creating.

Ed didn't feel that his product company competed with his service company. In fact, his ideas for the product business were going in a very different direction.

Ed went on to sell his company. And he made it very clear to his investment banker and all potential buyers that he was going to keep and grow the product side. He had the exit, recognized the value of his life's work, and redirected his energy and focus to his core passion—innovating. It was almost as though he reached the summit of his mountain and took a zip line to the mountain he really wanted to climb.

Entrepreneurs don't often retire as the rest of the world understands retirement. **More likely, they find they want to climb another mountain—some want to climb Everest, and some want an easier and more relaxed journey.** So they'll take on a smaller project or something they aren't as closely involved with.

Working with one owner on planning his life experience post his exit, he told me, "Ali, I don't want another child; I want grandchildren. If I do a new deal, I will be grandpa, and I'll find the right parent that can stay up through the night."

The beauty in what you have built to this point is that you get that optionality. You do not have to make it an all-or-nothing choice, either. Optionality allows you to trade all of your current success for just the portions of it that you love.

YOUR SECOND ACT

Expecting an entrepreneur to stop working after selling their company is like expecting an artist to stop painting because they sold enough art to retire.

When you have a passion for building something and creating a better solution, business is not just a way to make money—it's a way of life.

It is this passion that often prevents a business owner from ever selling their company.

If you do choose to sell, it will likely create a large void in your life. For many years, your business has served as a source of direction, focus, and commitment. You have subconsciously become very used to that feeling, and having it go away may be one of the hardest periods of your life.

With that being said, there is a new path, and if planned right, it'll be a better path.

Most entrepreneurs don't start their company based on their ultimate strengths, talents, and personal passion. They didn't do extensive market research on what industry to enter. They didn't have a detailed plan with market analysis and a crystal-clear map to conquer their industry. More likely, you were presented with an opportunity or came up with an idea or had a career that you thought you could do better on your own. You took the entrepreneurial leap because it just made sense.

You didn't need to have a perfect plan. You just had an appetite for risk and the perseverance to succeed.

And you did. Against all odds, you made magic happen.

Now it is time for your second act, and you have substantially more resources, knowledge, and experience, which can help propel you further and faster.

Being intentional as to what you want to pursue and why will be critical to creating your desired Return on Life Experience™.

There is a Japanese concept called ikigai (diagram below). Ikigai is "a reason for being," referring to having a direction or purpose in life, providing a sense of fulfillment, and toward which you can take action, giving you satisfaction and a sense of meaning.

Ikigai addresses the intersections of what you love, what the world needs, what you are good at, and what you can be paid for.

If you have enough financial resources that you do not need to get paid, your options of where you dedicate your time within the diagram are limitless. You might choose to pursue a new venture with large financial benefits or a truly altruistic passion project.

At this juncture, you get to think about what you want to do, what your unique talents and abilities are, and how you can leverage past success to gain an advantage on your future venture.

This post-exit choice can overwhelm many entrepreneurs. It can feel a little bit too powerful—a little too unrestricted. This often leads entrepreneurs to go right back to what they did before, or a variation of it.

In the second act, I encourage entrepreneurs to think about their personal competitive advantage and how they can use it to make their unique impact.

To shoot their arrow and paint the target around it.

There may be a thousand people who can build a company like the one you'll build next, but when it's the right company and you're the right person to do it, the competitive landscape changes. The chances of competing against someone else who has your skills, talents, passions, and strengths running that exact business will be much lower.

Your next step—one you can do right now, before anything else is set in motion—is to get to know yourself. Spend some time analyzing your strengths and weaknesses, your personality profiles, and your unique talents. For all of the time that we spend thinking about what you want, take just as much time to think about who you are and who you want to be.

Identifying what makes you unique and what makes you happy will further clarify what you really want and how to allocate your time. There are plenty of things you can find enjoyment in, but only a few things are truly your best and favorite.

You have an opportunity to start fresh, a clean slate to draw up your ideal life. Filled with what you love to do, with the skills you've acquired over the years, and with Independent Wealth to finance it...there's absolutely no limit to what you might do and how much enjoyment you can have.

CHAPTER 9

ASSET PROTECTION STRATEGY

A Good Defense Creates
a Better Offense

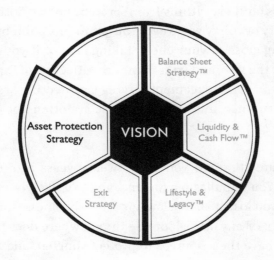

WHEN IT COMES TO ASSET PROTECTION, I'VE MET TWO TYPES OF business owners. Those who have seen or experienced risk exposure—whether through a lawsuit, a partnership that blew up, or an unexpected tragedy that was not planned for—and those who have not.

Their experiences usually drive their desire for planning. For some, asset protection is the number-one goal on their list; for others, it's an expense that they avoid as much as possible. Unfortunately, avoidance doesn't make the threat actually go away.

Many owners are driving at ninety miles an hour down the highway with no seat belt on, saying that their windshield will keep them safe.

This component may be difficult to grasp for the same reasons that your plans haven't changed in years. Most highly successful owners built everything from scratch and had nothing at all just twenty or thirty years ago. You got to this point by holding everything close to your chest, taking care of it yourself, and assuming the risk, and your plans are reflective of that. Creating a downside management strategy, protecting assets, paying for insurance, and mitigating risk are often not your first priority.

But you aren't where you were twenty years ago. A lot has changed. You've built up a fortune, and you likely want to protect it. If you lose it all to a lawsuit, a new business venture that goes south, or any other looming threat, where does that leave you? You have the resources to protect yourself, and all things considered, you would rather have a plan—and not just for yourself but for all those you support and love.

The WISE™ Asset Protection Strategy addresses the following questions:

- Looking at my total position, what are the major risks that I am exposed to?

- What assets are protected by law?

- How do I best position my assets?

- What risks should I retain versus insure or protect?

- Do I need to buy insurance?

- How do I protect the assets passed to my family?

- If I am sued, what's my exposure?

Some people reach this point still unsure whether they need any kind of asset protection or risk management plan. Others are looking for the special offshore plan with all the bells and whistles.

WISE takes you to a place of clarity, starting with education.

One WISE concept creates a simple asset protection overview with a three-light system: red, yellow, and green. Since the graphic is in black and white here, you'll have to visualize the colors.

On the left is the red light, where your assets are exposed. In the middle is the yellow light, where your assets are deterrents, or are somewhat protected. On the right side is the green light, where your assets are protected by either state law or federal law. This will vary from state to state and country to country, if you are not in the US. Looking at your Total Balance Sheet through this lens allows you to see your exposure and gain perspective.

You could build an entire strategy to take advantage of asset protection benefits provided by law, without having to go through hoops like moving assets offshore or putting something into a complex structure.

For some, you may *want* to use complex structures, and that's something you can address with your advisor team. I'll explain how to create the best model for effective advisor team collaboration in Chapter 11.

Additionally, you'll need to identify the key risks and issues with your overall financial position. Business agreements, corporate entities, and insurance should all be reviewed based on your current position and risk exposure. Then those risks can be prioritized based on your goals. Having clarity to the issue and the exposure will motivate a plan to fill the critical gaps and make sure you have a plan for the unforeseen.

For many owners, you are heavily invested in an illiquid business interest. Consider what would happen if you didn't wake up tomorrow morning. How does that affect your family? Your business? Your legacy? What is the tax exposure?

The story goes that George Steinbrenner faced a dilemma that many entrepreneurs eventually do—but on a much bigger scale. He, of course, was the owner of the New York Yankees, with an estimated value of over $1 billion. The problem was that his estate—at least the New York Yankees part of it—was highly illiquid.

When his advisors reviewed his position, they informed George that the estate tax to his heirs would be over $400 million dollars. Potentially forcing an asset sale or creating less than ideal circumstances for the family to raise capital and pay the IRS.

A similar concern might apply to a landowner whose estate includes $100 million worth of land that had been acquired throughout their lifetime. If that's you, when you pass, your heirs will owe a sizable estate tax (currently 40 percent of that value), regardless of how easy or hard it is to access that sum.

This is true of all assets, art, buildings, businesses, stock—illiquidity can quickly turn into risk, no matter how secure those assets seem to be.

Luckily for Steinbrenner, his advisors helped assess this risk and gave guidance on how to protect it.

He wanted the Yankees to stay in the family, and the idea was to buy insurance on his life to cover the estate tax, or a large part of it. Coming up with $400 million would be a huge undertaking; however, he could afford to pay premiums on a life insurance policy, and the eventual proceeds would be a source of tax-free liquidity for his heirs.

The premiums on life insurance (that his family certainly didn't need for traditional insurance purposes) covered the tax bill they couldn't pay otherwise.

Incidentally, he happened to die in 2010, the one year in almost 100 years when there was no estate tax. So his heirs kept the insurance payout *and* skipped the estate tax. In short, he had effective planning and impeccable timing.

Sometimes protection is for peace of mind, and sometimes it is a lifesaver, but in either case, it is good practice to protect what you have built. WISE and your Asset Protection Strategy provide a framework to assess, prioritize, and solve the key risks and exposures you face as an owner.

CHAPTER 10

LIFETIME TAX STRATEGY™

*It's Not What You Make
but What You Keep That Matters*

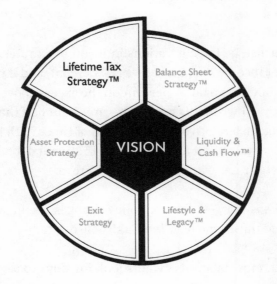

WHAT'S YOUR LARGEST BILL? YOUR MORTGAGE? YOUR TRAVEL budget? Your plane?

Nope, it's your tax bill. And if not now, then it will be when you sell your company, when you pass away, or when you get audited.

That's why it's not what you make but what you keep that matters. All business owners learned this concept early on when we first measured the difference between gross revenue and net profit.

Philosophically speaking, taxes can serve a great purpose. They provide shared resources such as schools, roads, infrastructure, defense, etc. However, the code is not simple. There are sales taxes, property taxes, income taxes, franchise taxes, gift taxes, and even a death or estate tax when you pass away. Furthermore, due to things like special interest groups, tax loopholes, and inefficient spending, the tax system can become very unfair and imbalanced.

There can also be large gyrations in income tax rates. In 1980, the highest income tax bracket was 70 percent, and if you made over $215,000, you paid 70 percent on the excess above that level. At the time I write this book, rates are about half that level. A huge change in a relatively short period of time. With high government spending and a rising level of national debt, it's quite likely that tax rates will increase in the future.

Sadly, the easy targets for tax policy changes are high-income earners and those who have built a sizable estate.

As a result, most business owners look for ways to save money for April 15 each year. But only looking at your annual tax liability on a year-by-year basis is quite limiting and often highly inefficient.

The sixth and final component of WISE is having a Lifetime Tax Strategy. The Lifetime Tax Strategy focuses on minimizing the amount of tax you pay over your lifetime, consistent with your goals and vision, divided into a Strategic Tax Plan and a Tactical Tax Plan.

The strategic tax plan supports your long-term Balance Sheet Strategy and how you position assets over many years to minimize tax. This might include what investments you select, what entity you choose for your company or companies, or your portfolio strategy. This is your Strategic Game Plan for growing your wealth while managing taxes.

The Tactical Tax Plan focuses on what you are doing in a specific year. This might include capital gain transactions, charitable donations, property tax payments, depreciation, gain or loss harvesting, or timing of your income recognition.

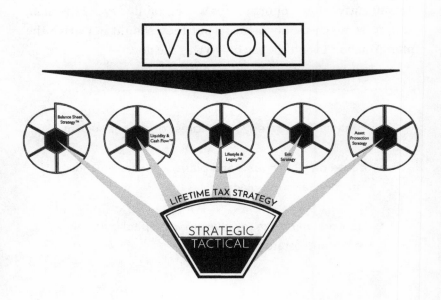

Simply put, you are looking at your balance sheet the way a private equity firm might look at a business. How can we shift different components to help generate more value?

However, the reason that a Lifetime Tax Strategy is the final component of WISE is because tax strategies should support your overall vision.

There are few people I've met who tell me their vision is to avoid paying taxes. I don't believe that to be true even for them, and if it is, they are the exception. You want to build your Balance Sheet Strategy, your Lifestyle & Legacy, your Exit Strategy, and all the components within WISE based on your vision. Once you have that vision, you can integrate the tax strategies that support it.

Tax incentives and opportunities will certainly *impact* the plan, and, in some cases, augment it, but they should not drive the plan. You don't want the tax tail to wag the dog.

Your Lifetime Tax Strategy will address questions such as:

- Based on all my goals and plans, what are my most effective tax strategies?

- How do I minimize my investment capital gain, income, and estate taxes?

- How do I minimize tax when I sell my company?

- What are the pros and cons of different tax structures?

- How does my charitable vision affect my tax planning?

- Am I missing out on any special tax incentives?

- How can I integrate my overall goals to create less tax?

- How do I create a plan to hedge against future tax increases?

- How do I make sure that I'm not leaving money on the table?

CREATING A LIFETIME TAX STRATEGY™

Having a Balance Sheet Strategy and your goals for Lifestyle & Legacy identified allows you to have more levers to create a tax strategy.

The beauty of the Lifetime Tax Strategy is that it generally doesn't impact your investment risk but can substantially increase net returns.

If you're growing your balance sheet at 10 percent per year, between everything you own, you may net 6 percent after taxes. And after you factor in estate taxes, you might only net 4 percent of the original 10 percent.

However, by having a Lifetime Tax Strategy in place, that same 10 percent return may generate a 7 percent net return after taxes. The difference of 3 percent higher net returns is enormous.

Building out a Lifetime Tax Strategy creates outperformance through asset positioning, not asset risk—enabling you to generate higher net return.

In other words, you can own the same business, real estate, or index fund you would have otherwise but net much more.

Here is a simple example as it relates to investment income tax. We know that certain assets are going to be taxed at different rates. If you own a corporate bond fund, income is taxed at ordinary income tax rates, which are currently around 40 percent.

If you take that same bond fund and put it in an IRA, there's no annual taxation. Wouldn't it make sense to put all your highly taxed bonds in an IRA? Then outside the IRA, have your long-term stock funds that can receive preferential tax treatment at almost half the tax rate?

As opposed to having each account you own allocated at 60 percent stocks, 40 percent bonds, you could position the funds in the account with the most favorable tax treatment.

Same overall risk, different net return.

When you know your Exit Strategy—sale or succession—you can select the best entity and plan to minimize the tax upon that sale. I've met owners who spent years building their company, then got to the signing table to sell it, only to realize their lack of planning resulted in double taxation on the sale of their company. Resulting in almost half of the company's value being lost to taxes.

The same goes for your Lifestyle & Legacy goals. If you have excess wealth that you will not need for your lifestyle, but you will leave as part of your legacy, you can reposition those assets for their ultimate purpose. By doing so now, you can save potentially millions of dollars in estate tax later.

LIFETIME TAX STRATEGY™ IN ACTION

Ten years ago, a business owner named Ralph came to me for consulting. He had a $50 million estate. He and his wife, Shelley, knew they needed an estate plan but didn't know how to approach it. They wanted to plan for the estate tax, and they had adult children who would eventually be given the estate, but they didn't want to release any of the funds to them yet.

I asked Ralph and Shelley a few questions: Do you know how much is enough for your financial independence? Do you know your long-term cash flow needs? Do you have charitable goals? Do you have a strategy for your business exit or succession?

Their answers were not clear, and there was no defined plan. They needed much more than an estate plan or a will; they needed more clarity on their goals and an integrated strategy to bring all the pieces together.

As I guided them through the first five components of WISE, we were able to determine that they needed $30 million of the estate for their financial independence, which left a $20 million excess that would eventually go to family, charity, or the government, as everything eventually does.

Since they had already decided that they wanted to leave money for their children, they transferred all $20 million of their excess shares to a trust that would eventually be released to the children.

Now, ten years down the road, their business and estate has grown to over $150 million, and the children's trust is worth $60 million—with all of it safely free from the 40 percent estate tax that it would have otherwise been subject to.

That intentional decision—to reposition funds based on what they were for—resulted in a net tax savings of $24 million (and counting).

With the large growth in the estate, Ralph and Shelley have new plans to donate a substantial amount to charity. Because they know their Lifestyle & Legacy goals, they are able to take immediate income tax deductions on their charitable gifts, realizing significant savings on their tax bill, as well as ensuring the assets will go to the charities of their choice.

This is an example of what it looks like to create a Lifetime Tax Strategy.

Yes, tax savings are a factor that can help you accomplish your goals. But everything that you really want—the legacy you want to leave, the life you want to live, the next opportunities you want to take advantage of—is much bigger than the tax code.

All of your excess wealth will end up going to one of three outlets: family, charity, or the government. It's best to make that decision now rather than having it made for you later.

PART 3

DECISION

CHAPTER 11

THE WEALTH WITH PURPOSE® PROCESS

The Clear Path to Intentionality and Integration

WE HAVE REVIEWED ALL THE MAJOR ASPECTS of entrepreneurial wealth and placed everything into the six components of WISE™, representing all of your life's wealth. You're probably wondering, "How does it all come together *for me*?" This is a lot of information, and it involves several people and some heavy lifting to bring it together.

To do that much analysis, coordination, integration, and planning would be a huge ask on the business owner, and likely far from your highest and best use. To keep the solution as simple as possible for the owner, we have established a proven process to bring your Blueprint together.

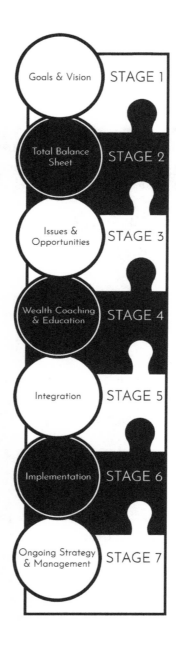

Wealth with Purpose is a core process within WISE to bring all the concepts together specifically for your position. There are three key benefits and outcomes generated by the process: it gives you the time and space to get clear about your goals, creates a blueprint to identify your priorities and strategies, and establishes collaboration to integrate your team of advisors.

WISE tools and concepts help with different aspects of your planning; the Wealth with Purpose process is the place where they integrate. The central process where all the pieces come together and an entrepreneur can plan and manage their life's wealth.

You can complete this process with a Guide, or you can self-manage the process. We will discuss both options in Chapter 12.

Think of the process like a chef preparing a meal: simply having the right ingredients is not enough. To get the right outcome, you need to complete each item in a particular order and at a particular time. You can't marinate the meat after you cook it, and you can't put a frozen turkey in the oven.

Having executed this process hundreds of times, I can tell you that skipping a step, doing it in the wrong order, or shortcutting the process will often lead to negative or a less than optimal result. However, using the correct steps and approach can create a new outcome altogether.

The Wealth with Purpose® process involves the following stages:

- Goals & Vision

- Total Balance Sheet™

- Issues & Opportunities

- Wealth Coaching & Education

- Integration

- Implementation

- Ongoing Strategy & Management

A Guide is there to ask the right questions, dig deep, and help your vision become clear.

STAGE ONE: GOALS & VISION

The first step involves setting initial goals and defining your vision for the future. There are countless planning strategies out there, especially for business owners. By clarifying your vision first—by knowing what you want—you simplify your potential solutions to a much smaller set. This will serve as your North Star. Every time you are in doubt, you can go back to this place to refocus on what you really want. **Starting with a clear vision and set of goals creates a much higher probability of success than looking at strategies first.** It also prevents analysis paralysis while analyzing which of a hundred different strategies you want to utilize.

Executing a plan without having a clear vision is like making side dishes for a meal without knowing what the main course is. As funny as that may sound, the reality is that most planning—especially when it comes to personal wealth—is done without creating an overall vision.

It's rare that I come across a business owner who has actually gone through an intentional planning process where their vision was the driving force behind the plan. Usually, plans are built by the most common solutions in the marketplace. I often hear an estate plan starting with "In order to minimize your tax, we can use a trust or a partnership; let's talk about them."

Investment strategy might be based on "What's your risk tolerance or target return?" Or "This law allows you to give this much to your kids tax-free, so you should do it." Or "This will protect your assets against creditors, so it makes sense."

That type of simplistic, paint-by-numbers planning does not incorporate the owner's vision or account for their unique circumstances.

Knowing the end goal starts with one question: "what do you want?"

This question opens the door, and so much follows from there.

When those big desires are clearly defined, other goals on sur-rounding issues can be determined. There is a difference be-tween an initial goal like:

- I want to pass my company to my children

And a refined goal of:

- I want to pass my company shares to my four children, with Rebecca being the CEO and having control, and

    * I want my other three children to have ownership as well as the option to sell stock at fair value if they want out

    * I want this to take place over the next ten years so I can be there to watch the process

    * I want my spouse and me to have financial inde-pendence separate from the company

    * I want to ensure that any assets passed to my chil-dren are protected from a future divorce or from creditors or lawsuits

    * I want to minimize potential family conflict

By making a decision about who leads the company, we can identify several supporting goals that can help create a plan.

These goals may relate to family succession, Independent Wealth™, legacy creation, estate planning, tax minimization, gifts to your children and grandchildren, charitable planning, and so on.

Defining the big picture helps us add goals to support it.

In my experience, goals will refine as you go through the process and gain more education on strategies and options. I constantly witness business owners enhancing their vision as they gain wealth coaching and education. So if you are intimidated to try and set your vision or life goals, don't stress—just put down what comes to mind and refine as you go along.

It's important not to procrastinate because of a desire to think about each step too deeply. You'll get plenty of time to do that as you go through the steps. Think about progress, not perfection.

STAGE TWO: TOTAL BALANCE SHEET™

The next step is developing an accurate, centralized, Total Balance Sheet. It shocks me how many business owners, even with multimillion-dollar net worths, do not have a Total Balance Sheet. I don't mean down to the perfect penny, but we need to know what every asset is and where every asset is.

Today, most professional advisors operate with insufficient data. Most business owners don't have a Total Balance Sheet, a reasonable business valuation, or a list of all assets that their attorney, CPA, financial advisor, and everybody else works from.

Usually, all the different advisors are working from different data sets pulled together at different times and from different sources—and they are often inaccurate and out of date.

For example, a business owner might have created a net worth statement for their bank when they applied for a loan. The CPA may have their tax returns. Maybe their financial advisor has a list of all their investment accounts. But that's really not good enough. We need a Total Balance Sheet that has all assets listed—including a reasonable valuation of the company, all personal property, and a full estate layout including insurance policies and the values of assets within and outside of the estate (outside of estate assets might be trusts of assets passed to the children).

Business owners who do have that information often don't share it with their team of professionals. And, to be fair, there isn't necessarily a high demand from those advisors to see it. But without it, your team of professionals is working from incomplete data.

I've seen wills drafted without the lawyer even seeing a balance sheet or knowing the true business value and estate tax exposure. In one case, I met a business owner who had a company worth over $100 million. Their attorney had drafted a great will and medical directives; however, they had no plan whatsoever to address the $40-million-plus estate tax. In this particular case, the business owner was divorced with three children, and if they were to pass away, there would be an immediate estate tax liability.

When we talked with the attorney and showed him an accurate balance sheet, he was floored. He had no idea that the company was that valuable and, as a result, did not think through the repercussions of the estate tax. This was perhaps the most impactful part of their entire wealth plan, and it had been overlooked because of a lack of clear data.

In other cases, I've seen large charitable donations made without any use of appreciated stock or real estate, resulting in tens or hundreds of thousands in lost money. To further explain, if you are going to make a large charitable donation, it is usually best to donate appreciated assets, like real estate or stocks, resulting in an income tax deduction in addition to avoiding capital gain taxes. In essence, double tax savings.

It's critical that you gather complete and accurate data, and that everybody on your team works from the same data set. Addressing it all together creates more opportunities and levers for planning. It creates alignment, allowing your team to see your position through the same lens. It also gives you an opportunity to see everything you have in one place, and that can be an enjoyable and reflective process in and of itself.

Once the Total Balance Sheet is complete, it can be integrated with the tools and concepts within WISE. You can view your actual Investment Opportunity Diagram™, seeing your concentrations between business, real estate, securities, and cash. You can view your Lifestyle & Legacy™ Capital, seeing your assets allocated for Independent Wealth, for fun, for your children, or for charity. You can see your Liquidity Buckets™, giving you clarity over your excess. All these items together will give you a lens to view your position more clearly, creating perspective for a better and more holistic decision.

A business owner using WISE said it best during a balance sheet collaboration meeting: "Looking at all of this makes me feel like I am treating my personal wealth like it's a business. I can see everything in one place, and it makes decisions so much easier."

STAGE THREE: ISSUES & OPPORTUNITIES

The next step is to clearly identify the key issues and opportunities that need to be addressed. **If an owner doesn't recognize or understand the issues they are facing, there won't be a sense of urgency to take action.**

When we have clear issues, there's an incentive for the business owner to prioritize them and work with their team to build out a plan.

After the issues are identified, we also need to have buy-in from every member of the team. And by team, I mean your tax, legal, and financial advisors, etc.

Many times, a plan will turn sideways when there is a conflict over a perceived issue that the attorney, CPA, investment advisor, financial planner, or business owner disagree on. Not having buy-in from everyone on the same set of issues will mean each team member will be trying to solve a different problem, and that can create more gaps and issues. It will create misalignment, additional cost, unnecessary analysis, and extra fees. You will end up wasting a lot of time and money while not getting to the right solution.

It's necessary to have a clear list of issues laid out so that everyone sees the same points. Everyone on the advisor team and the owner must align on the issues they're working to solve, while using the owner's goals as their North Star. This step is crucial in order to create the right alignment and urgency before moving to the next.

"Opportunities" are all the relevant things that could be considered. Owners hear about planning opportunities all the time, from their associations, seminars, articles, cocktail conversations, etc. Some of these opportunities are totally irrelevant, some are too good to be true, and some are great avenues for value enhancement.

The Issues & Opportunities list creates a place to capture these ideas and bring them to the table for discussion. Sometimes an idea is good, but it's not the right time, so it stays on the list for future consideration. Sometimes it's just an idea and can be removed if not relevant. The important thing is keeping a place where relevant issues and opportunities can be addressed in the right way.

STAGE FOUR: WEALTH COACHING & EDUCATION

Wealth coaching and education are so important during the planning process, and they are often overlooked. Business owners usually build their wealth using a few methods that they know and know well. Over time, they stick with what works and dismiss the rest. Paradigms form—some good and some bad.

The wealth coaching and education allow for those paradigms to be revisited, sometimes changed, and, at the least, identified and worked with. As a result, the business owner may be open to solutions that weren't previously on the table but are aligned with their vision. Through education, they can expand their tools beyond just the hammer and the screwdriver they had been using for years and now have a full tool belt, and maybe even a toolbox.

Your opinions on different approaches, tools, and planning ideas are formed by your life experiences and philosophies. **Wealth coaching and education give you the opportunity to revisit those philosophies with a new lens.** Understanding your Paradigm of Money™, Point C™, your new normal, control, risk, nonretirement, the Investment Opportunity Diagram, Entrepreneur's Opportunity Cost, the six components of WISE, and your desires for Return on Life Experience™ can shift the way you see your wealth as well as the specific tools you use to manage it.

And wealth coaching is not a one-time process but something that is continually revisited and enhanced. I have found that business owners will attend the same Re-investment Dilemma™ workshop multiple times and have a different takeaway or paradigm shift from the content.

As you reflect on how you got here, what you want, your options, and what others have used successfully, your personal ideas will evolve and become clearer. Wealth coaching and education provide the framework and time to address these items.

STAGE FIVE: INTEGRATION

The next step is fostering effective integration and collaboration. Having a team of experts is really important, but **effective collaboration will turn a team of experts into one expert team.** That's what every business owner wants, both within their business and for their personal wealth. When that happens, the output can be exponentially greater than when each professional is working in a silo.

Think about it this way: if you met someone that had a $50 million company and their leadership team had never met each other, you would probably think they were crazy. Similarly, if you have a $50 million balance sheet and you are not having your personal tax, legal, and financial advisors meet or collaborate, you are likely missing out on opportunities or making costly mistakes.

Effective integration begins with the different advisors aligning at the same table, or nowadays, Zoom meeting. For most business owners, this group meeting is happening for the first time in their history.

Next, they need a clear description of the business owner's vision and goals, a Total Balance Sheet, a list of all the issues and opportunities, a purposeful agenda, and a Guide to facilitate and quarterback the meeting.

When they meet, they will all have the same information and can align around goals, issues, and opportunities. This creates much more efficiency and allows them to get on the same page quickly.

A business owner might have ten issues to solve, with two or three major issues at the top of the list. Oftentimes, if you solve the big issue, a lot of the ancillary issues go away.

That's the magic behind an effective collaborative process. You and your team can see all the issues and opportunities at the same time and create strategies that solve multiple issues.

I remember one meeting where an owner had been debating buying a life insurance policy for payment of estate taxes, but through his collaboration meeting, a creative estate planning idea was brought to the table that completely eliminated his need for insurance. That approach solved multiple issues and also saved him substantial, unnecessary insurance premiums.

Since no one person has a monopoly on good ideas and things are always changing, collaboration creates a platform to capture your best strategies and fully utilize your team.

Having an initial collaboration meeting separate from the business owner allows for a faster and more efficient process. Professionals can speak their language, resolve conflicts, and hash out technical issues.

After that first meeting, there may be follow-up meetings, usually involving the entire advisor team and the business owner. These meetings will be a lot more focused than the initial collaboration because they've already filtered out the multiple options and reduced them down to ones that really fit the owner's vision and goals.

These meetings often create exponential value. The framework does the heavy lifting in advance, so the professionals can really be strategic on solutions and efficient with their time. Because WISE is so comprehensive, there are many levers that can be utilized, resulting in ideas and outcomes that create enhanced value for the business owner.

The Wealth with Purpose® Blueprint

The next step is to capture everything in one Blueprint. At this point, you will have much more clarity on your goals. You'll have increased education on options, alignment of your advisors, innovative strategies to enhance value, and documentation for action and continuity. The output of this entire process is captured in your Wealth with Purpose Blueprint—essentially a business plan for your personal wealth.

The Blueprint will address the six components of WISE, key issues and opportunities, a Total Balance Sheet, and your vision, goals, and actions. All coming together to create purpose behind your wealth.

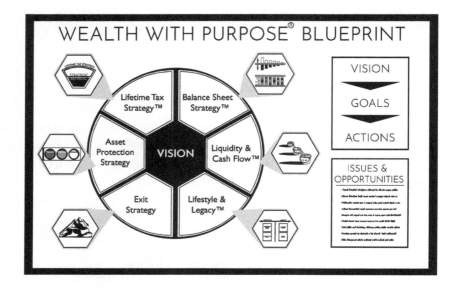

STAGE SIX: IMPLEMENTATION

The Blueprint is laid out, and you know where you're going and why. It's now time to implement. The number of items to be implemented will vary substantially based on your situation, goals, and complexity.

In order to effectively implement your strategies, **you need to determine the necessary actions, accountable parties, and deadlines**.

It sounds simple, but how many times have you started working on something and not seen it reach the finish line?

This process creates a visible list of actions and deadlines from which you can establish status updates to ensure execution.

Implementation will include items such as establishing a trust, changing your business entity, reallocating your investment accounts, establishing a charitable entity, or even beginning the process of selling your company.

Implementation can involve a few or many steps, depending on your plan. Once implementation is in motion, there will likely be a huge sense of relief, and many aspects of your planning will be complete.

It's important to note that some issues and opportunities will be immediately addressed; others will take time and thought before action. That brings us to Stage 7, Ongoing Strategy & Management.

STAGE SEVEN: ONGOING STRATEGY & MANAGEMENT

Once the plan is implemented, there is a structure for ongoing strategy and management that needs to be established to continue progress, measure results, and accommodate for change. **Just like with a business plan, planning is not done once, put on a shelf, and then revisited years later. It's an ongoing, dynamic process.** Your Blueprint is going to adjust with changes in the tax law, changes in your business income, changes in your family situation, and changes in your goals.

Ongoing strategy and management involve periodic meetings to proactively measure your progress and execute upon your goals. Often, adjustments happen as business owners develop new goals or have a shift in strategy. It's very important to be proactive with planning and have accountability checkpoints that measure results.

Here are some of the items to consider within an ongoing management strategy:

- Have your goals changed?

- How has your plan performed?

- What changes have taken place in the marketplace or tax law?

- Updating the values of your balance sheet

- Reassessing your strategy as it relates to all six components of WISE

- Tracking your progress toward your goals

And here is an example of a schedule of meetings to support an ongoing management strategy:

- Q1: Balance Sheet Strategy™ Meeting:

    * Update and review all assets on the balance sheet, business values, investments values, performance, etc.

* Address relevant Issues & Opportunities

* Distribute action items.

- Q2: Meet with CPA and CFO on tax preparation

- Q3: Wealth with Purpose Blueprint Meeting

    * Review and update vision and goals

    * Review of all components of WISE

    * Address relevant Issues & Opportunities

    * Distribute action items

- Q4: Tax Strategy Meeting

    * Review all taxable income streams for the year

    * Create a year-end tactical tax strategy for all assets and income

    * Address relevant Issues & Opportunities

    * Distribute action items

Depending on your goals and the size of your estate, this may happen in one annual meeting or break up into several meetings. The key thing is that all of the important issues are addressed and there is movement from intention to action.

At this point, you've learned about all the different stages in the Wealth with Purpose process and the goal behind each stage.

Over the past decade, hundreds of business owners have been taken through this process, and it's proven to deliver enhanced results encompassing every major area of planning.

As with the rest of this process, you have different options on how you execute your plan. You may be interested in having a Guide to help you through this process, you may be looking for workshop-based guidance, or you may be looking for content to self-manage.

In any situation, **what's important is that you take action toward capturing your success and creating (and executing) an intentional plan.** My goal is to provide you with the tools, insight, and knowledge to take those steps. It is your choice as to which path you would like to take.

In the next chapter, I will provide an overview of the content and different ways you can start using the Wealth Integration System for Entrepreneurs™ to take control of your dilemmas and your planning.

CHAPTER 12

GETTING WISE™

Your Path to Taking Control

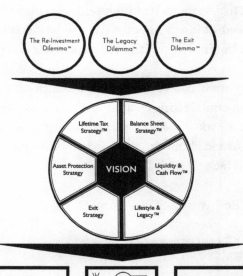

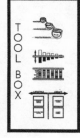

Once upon a time, you started your company in hopes of building something of your own—providing yourself and your family with the financial independence and security that you desire and pursuing an opportunity to create a better outcome.

And after years of perseverance, you've arrived. You've built a level of wealth that you likely once only dreamed of, and you now have choices and options that you might not have thought possible.

Your relentless perseverance in building your company will now have to shift to also include more intentional planning. **Treating your personal balance sheet with the same intention that you do your business is critical to capturing your life's work.**

Through this book, you've learned that wealth is not the end but a means to an end. Getting clear about what you want from your wealth will take you closer to that ultimate goal, whatever it may be. You've learned about the three critical dilemmas that entrepreneurs will face on their journey:

- The Re-investment Dilemma™

- The Legacy Dilemma™

- The Exit Dilemma™

In the Re-investment Dilemma, a business owner faces the challenge of where to re-invest their excess capital—back in their company, in real estate, in the stock market, in cash...What path should an owner take?

The Entrepreneur's Investment Opportunity Diagram™ gives you a way to visualize and map out your investment opportunities and understand the pros and cons to each. It reminds you that investments should not be made purely from a standpoint of return on investment but also factor in items such as opportunity cost, control, risk, liquidity, and the impact on your core focus.

What's important to remember here is that your investment choice is not about making a right or wrong decision. It's about the right decision for *you*, and giving you the clarity and perspective so that you can make an informed decision based on both the financial impact as well as the life impact.

The Legacy Dilemma is equally challenging, and, in most cases, even more emotional. What is it all for—for you, for children, for charity, for fun? What do you do with all that you've built?

Here, you learned about Lifestyle & Legacy Capital and how to separate the capital that you need for financial independence and for fun from the excess capital that may be destined for family, charity, or, if you don't plan well, the government.

The framework allows you to be more intentional and create different categories for your capital and allocate each according to their end goal versus treating everything as one group.

You can simplify the decisions to be led by your vision and goals. Reducing the chance that you get lost in the complexity of tax and legal jargon.

We also addressed how leadership succession for your company could make the largest impact on your legacy, and the importance of establishing and enabling a clear successor. Always remembering that succession is not an event or a document but a process that happens over several years.

The Exit Dilemma addressed the critical decision of what you should do with your company—grow it, sell it, pass it on to your child, or perhaps sell the company to your executive team or employees.

The Exit Dilemma can be the most life-impacting—you learned about how 75 percent of entrepreneurs profoundly regretted selling their company one year after their exit.

Business owners don't just invest in a business because of return on investment. They invest in a business because it's a passion, a calling, and, in many cases, a way of life.

Knowing your desired life experience, having clarity over how you want to spend your time, knowing what you need for financial independence, and knowing what might come next will all aid in the decision of whether you should exit your company and how.

You've also learned that Entrepreneurs Don't Retire™—we simply find a new passion to pursue. It is critical to identify your personal passion and create a path forward before exiting your business. As in the mountain climbing example, 80 percent of the accidents don't happen on the way up. They happen on the way down. Treat the life after the sale of your company with intentionality and time.

These three dilemmas are the most critical, but they are not alone. This book has outlined many different stories and examples of how they manifest for business owners, as there are many other financial decisions, life decisions, and dilemmas associated with the entrepreneurial journey.

You have learned about the six components of the Wealth Integration System for Entrepreneurs and how everything within an entrepreneur's wealth fits into one of those six components. WISE addresses all the various dilemmas and decisions at the top level, providing a framework to think through and get clarity over your personal wealth.

You've also learned about the Wealth with Purpose process that brings the specific WISE components together with your team of professionals. Creating clarity on the purpose behind your wealth as well as integrating your planning and professional advisors.

You've learned about the path to create the best possible outcome with the fewest steps—now it's time to get started.

GETTING STARTED

One of the common questions I receive here is "At what point should I start looking at all of this?"

Perhaps Stephen Covey's most famous quote applies here:

> Begin with the end in mind.

The moment you have a successful business that's generating profits and cash flow, at the point where you can make considerations about where to re-invest your capital, it is beneficial to get WISE and learn about the impact it can make on your future decisions.

If you're Justin (from Chapter 1) with a $50 million company, you're way past due on getting started. If you have a successful business and you're already thinking about these dilemmas, start now. Getting clarity on your options and path is only going to accelerate your outcome.

That brings us to our next question: "what are my options on how to get started?"

You have learned a lot in this book, and chances are the concepts have already reframed your thinking about your decisions. You can use the learnings and approaches in this book to immediately impact your planning.

My goal is to help you maximize your success and have it create the life experience that you desire.

If you are looking for additional help and guidance, there are three potential paths you can take.

1. **If you're looking for more education** and want to stay connected, visit us online at WISEGlobalNetwork. com to get the latest resources and tools, complete the free WISE assessment, and learn about new content, courses, podcasts, and videos. We are constantly

creating and evolving to best serve our business owner community.

2. **If you are looking to self-manage** and implement WISE and want to gain independent guidance and perspective to help you go deeper, take a look at our content and courses. This is where you can gain in-depth education, step-by-step approaches, and perspective on how to address every aspect of WISE.

3. **If you are looking for a Guide™** to help you bring it all together, you have two choices.

   a. **You can join a workshop program with a group Guide.** I coach and facilitate immersive group workshops where you can learn and collaborate with other business owners, talking through different topics like The Three Dilemmas™ or the six components of WISE. For more information, visit WISEGlobalNetwork.com/workshops.

   b. **You can hire a solo Guide. As Dan Sullivan would say,** if you are looking for who, not how, you can engage a solo Guide to take you through WISE. You can do this in addition to the workshop program. To find your Guide and access resources, visit WISEGlobalNetwork.com/guide

If you haven't already completed the WISE Assessment to help you gain clarity on your starting point, be sure to visit WISEGlobalNetwork.com/assessment.

CONNECTING WITH ME

I welcome questions and feedback. If there's an open question you still have after reading this book—a piece of feedback or something that hasn't been addressed—I encourage you to contact me. Your question might be the topic of a future podcast, it might be a new tool that we create, or it may just be an opportunity for us to connect.

I love hearing from business owners and feel that the future success of our education and resource company is through your feedback. You can email me at feedback@wiseglobalnetwork.com.

If you would like to connect on any of my social channels, or if you are interested in speaking engagements, visit AliNasser.com to get all the information.

Additionally, you can access more information and expanded content from the book, including tools, resources, and videos, by visiting AliNasser.com/book.

As I mentioned in my note to you at the beginning of this book, my passion and my mission in writing this content is to help create better outcomes for every business owner who reads it.

My hope is that the concepts, principles, and approach that I have displayed within this book help you think more intentionally, have better perspective, and, at the end of the day, help you take action toward your best path forward.

Entrepreneurs really are my favorite people on the planet. And I'm always looking for ways to further connect and grow together.

With gratitude,

Ali Nasser

ABOUT THE AUTHOR

ALI NASSER IS A PASSIONATE ENTREPRENEUR, COMMUNICATOR, and life enthusiast. He loves helping people find their best path forward and enhancing intentionality. He spends his time guiding business owners in navigating the intersection of wealth and life planning.

Ali believes that wealth is a means, not an end. And by having the right framework to think about wealth and life decisions, you can find the outcome and impact you truly desire. His mission is to help owners gain *better perspective* so they can make *better decisions*, capturing their success and creating the life experience they truly desire.

Ali is a sought-after communicator and keynote speaker. He has shared his insights with audiences at a variety of institutions, workshops, and conferences, including Entrepreneurs' Organization, Vistage, and the EOS National Conference.

Ali has a degree in finance from the University of Houston's Bauer School of Business and taught at Rice University for seven years. He is a CERTIFIED FINANCIAL PLANNER™ (CFP), Certified Exit Planning Advisor (CEPA), and an Accredited Estate Planner (AEP).

Ali's life mission is to utilize entrepreneurial thinking to enable people and communities globally to pursue their passions and live better lives.

He lives in Houston, Texas.

For more information or to connect, visit AliNasser.com.

ABOUT
WISE GLOBAL NETWORK

THE WEALTH INTEGRATION SYSTEM FOR ENTREPRENEURS (WISE) is an education and content company created by entrepreneurs, for entrepreneurs.

The WISE mission is to provide business owners with *better perspective* so they can make *better decisions*. Through intentional coaching, immersive workshops, and a community of like-minded business owners, WISE creates experiences that enable you to define the vision for your wealth and life and design the pathway to capture your success.

WISEGlobalNetwork.com

ACKNOWLEDGMENTS

THIS BOOK TOOK MANY YEARS TO COMPLETE, AND THERE IS NO way it would have been possible without the help of so many people. I truly appreciate all of your support.

FAMILY AND FRIENDS

Mom, thank you for inspiring me and showing me how anything is possible if I take action.

Dad, thank you for teaching me humility and kindness.

Brooke, thank you for always believing in me and pushing me to find my best path in life.

Sina Tazehzad, thank you for being my best friend.

My Entrepreneurs Organization Forum: James McDonough, Rob Shaw, Mike Ecklund, Trent Staggers, Allie Danziger, Adam

Goldman, and Aman Dhuka. Thank you all for being my thought partners and sounding board through all the transitions.

MENTORS

Mahesh Desai—thank you for showing me my blind spots and having faith in my abilities.

Larry Kachler—thank you for teaching me to think about my business as an enterprise and not a practice.

Sina Tazehzad—thank you for being there in good times and bad and for the countless conversations on strategy.

Bill Kretlow—thank you for being the best finance professor any student could ask for.

Gino Wickman—thank you for your guidance and for inspiring me to create a greater impact.

Dan Sullivan—thank you for helping me think bigger and to find my Unique Ability®.

Stephen Covey—thank you for teaching me some of life's greatest habits.

Tom Haught—thank you for your guidance, insights, and mentorship.

COLLABORATORS, TEAM, AND CLIENTS

My manuscript collaborators: Mark C. Winters, Howard Rambin, Jeff Holler, Gino Wickman, Melissa Bushman, Amber Vilhauer, Lorie Clements, Vimal Kothari, Joseph Bramante, Alex Freytag, Bill Boyar, Jorge Squier, Amin Dhalla, James McDonough, Asif Dakri, Brett Berly, Jagdish Desai, Jay Jacobs, Cory Jackson, Rick Wilson, Raza Jafferi, Joe St. Thomas, Dave Spray, Chris Winkler, Kary Oberbrunner, Cameron Herold, and Ali Nadimi. Thank you all for taking the time to read my manuscript and provide such valuable feedback. This book would not be where it is without you.

To all my team members, present and past, that have helped make this book happen. Without you, none of this would be possible: Melissa Bushman, Kayllie Cooper Felske, Joseph St. Thomas, Lynsey Bergeron Honey, Sara-Katherine Johnson, Jared Waldrup, Carolina Tagmeyer, Sue Ellen Burch, Yvette Wang, Jack Cowling, and Brannan Sirratt. Thank you all for your support and your patience as we got this to the finish line.

To all my clients—thank you for having trust in me and my team and for the insights and experiences that made this book possible.

Connect and collaborate with
other business owners facing similar
challenges and opportunities.

Gain perspective. Chart a path forward.
Achieve your desired outcomes.

LEARN MORE
WiseGlobalNetwork.com/Workshop